W9-DCZ-194

HORIZON

JANUARY, 1961 · VOLUME III, NUMBER 3

© 1960 by American Horizon, Inc. All rights reserved under Berne and Pan-American Copyright Conventions. Reproduction in whole or in part of any article without permission is prohibited. U. S. copyright is not claimed for pages 17-24 or for the color plates on pages 5-8, 12, 38-39, 42, 43, 50-55, 78, 79. Printed in the United States of America.

HORIZON
A Magazine of the Arts

JANUARY, 1961 • VOLUME III, NUMBER 3

PUBLISHER
James Parton

EDITOR
Joseph J. Thorndike, Jr.

MANAGING EDITOR
William Harlan Hale

ASSOCIATE EDITORS
Ralph Backlund
Robert Emmett Ginna

ASSISTANT EDITORS
Ada Pesin
Jane Wilson

CONTRIBUTING EDITOR
Margery Darrell

EDITORIAL ASSISTANTS
Shirley Abbott. Caroline Backlund,
Alan Doré, Katherine Mayor

COPY EDITOR
Mary Ann Pfeiffer
Assistants: Rita Resnikoff, Ruth H. Wolfe

ART DIRECTOR
Irwin Glusker
Assistant: Elton Robinson

ADVISORY BOARD
Gilbert Highet, *Chairman*
Frederick Burkhardt   Oliver Jensen
Marshall B. Davidson   Jotham Johnson
Richard M. Ketchum   John Walker

EUROPEAN CONSULTING EDITOR
J. H. Plumb
Christ's College, Cambridge

EUROPEAN BUREAU
Gertrudis Feliu, *Chief*
28 Quai du Louvre, Paris

CIRCULATION DIRECTOR
Richard V. Benson

HORIZON is published every two months by
American Horizon, Inc., a subsidiary of American
Heritage Publishing Co., Inc., 551 Fifth Avenue,
New York 17, N. Y.
    Single Copies: $3.95
Annual Subscriptions: $18.00 in the U.S. & Can.
        $19.00 elsewhere

Second-Class postage paid at New York, N.Y.

HORIZON welcomes contributions but can assume
no responsibility for such unsolicited material.

COVER: When the Chinese Nationalists left the mainland for Formosa in 1949, they took with them the vast Palace Museum Collection of art treasures. A detail from one of the finest of several thousand paintings in the collection—*Eight Riders in Spring*, attributed to the tenth-century master Chao Yen—appears here. Painted in ink and colors on silk, it shows a group of noblemen in colorful jackets riding through a palace courtyard. The figure at right, with whip raised, may be an emperor. This is one of the Formosa paintings coming to America this year (see the article, with portfolio, beginning on page 14). It appears in *Chinese Painting*, a recent Skira Art Book.

FRONTISPIECE: In this splendid drawing, *The Death of Seneca*, Giovanni Battista Tiepolo (1696–1770) irreverently dispenses with classical iconography. Instead of the devoted Roman disciples, he depicts a band of gallants dressed for a masque, casually looking at the aged philosopher who cut his own wrists when condemned for conspiracy by the Emperor Nero, his former pupil. Flooded with the light so dear to the Venetian heart, the pen and wash drawing is executed with the *brio* and glittering touch of the last Venetian master. It was a recent gift of the Joseph and Helen Regenstein Foundation to The Art Institute of Chicago.

THE SECRETS OF SAN MEN

A traveler from Red China reports how, neck and neck with the

builders of a vast dam on the Yellow River, scholars are racing

to illuminate the past and preserve the treasures of ancient China

Seven hundred miles above the delta where it fingers its way into the Yellow Sea, the Yellow River of China forces a passage between the precipitous rocks of San Men Gorge. Until recently, two islands divided the river there. High on the side of one of them, safe from the surging waters, inscriptions were carved by devout boatmen who, through many centuries, sought to reduce the peril of passing the fearsome place by honoring their earthly protectors and propitiating the river-gods. One such inscription was dedicated to the Great Yü, the semimythical emperor who is said to have founded the Hsia Dynasty in the twenty-third century B.C.

Who does not know the merits of the emperor; the whole world constantly resounds to the fame of the divine Yü. He ordered the water and the earth into their places; his praises are sung by the people in nine songs. He it was who chiseled away the mountain's bones so that we could sail the length of the river. . . .

Today, the work begun by the Great Yü is being completed—and he would marvel at it. For even as Yü caused the mountain's bones to be chiseled, modern engineers with dynamite have removed the islands and dammed the river.

The traditional name for the Yellow River is "China's Sorrow"; in the words are contained the *raison d'être* of the San Men Dam. According to the records and legends of three thousand years, some fifteen hundred floods have swept the lower reaches of the river, where today nearly two hundred million people live on the rice plains. The dam should end forever the unpredictable scourges of China's Sorrow.

The Communist government predicts that when the dam is completed in 1962, it will irrigate twenty million acres and will generate 1.2 million kilowatts for the industrial center that is envisaged for the area. But even as the new China is building, the old China is disappearing. Part of it will quite

On the facing page, Dr. Ling, deputy director of the archaeological team at San Men, displays a fine engraved bronze vessel of the Western Chou period. Above, a flag that was awarded for good work flies over the dam site where a construction team is leveling the gorge wall.

By NIGEL CAMERON
PHOTOGRAPHS BY BRIAN BRAKE

literally vanish beneath the lake that will stretch 160 miles upriver from the dam, inundating a thousand villages together with the sites and deposits of some of the earliest cultures of China. Accordingly, the Ministry of Culture in Peking and the Academia Sinica (China's national research academy) have launched a vast program to survey and record the archaeological treasures of the area to be flooded and to remove them to safety wherever feasible. (On a smaller scale the Chinese archaeological rescue project is similar to the one launched by UNESCO and the Egyptian government to preserve the monuments and deposits in the Nile region that will be flooded by the new Aswan Dam—Horizon, July,

1960). The Chinese archaeologists have already unearthed some extraordinary finds and amassed evidence of profound importance for scholars eager to illuminate the uncertain cultural history of ancient China.

In the history of early China the Yellow River played a role almost as central as that of the Nile in Egypt. But the early development of China was concentrated in a comparatively short section midway along the three-thousand-mile course of the river. In this cradle of Chinese civilization, stretching from Sian eastward for a couple of hundred miles to the vicinity of Loyang in Honan Province, the river cuts its way through a curious landscape that has been shaped and

The cave villages of the San Men region (left) have harbored the civilization of China for thousands of years. Dug into the hills along the Yellow River, they have been continuously occupied, each cave used until its walls crack, when a new cave is dug. This village will be inundated by the waters of the river seen in the background. At the dam site (below), an archaeologist takes a rubbing from an inscription carved in A.D. 1111 by boatmen about to essay the passage of the gorge. It is a eulogy to the Great Emperor Yü, who was celebrated for having made the river navigable.

OVERLEAF: The power of a ruler named Yuan T'u is evidenced by the burial of his five chariots and ten horses in a pit discovered with his tomb near San Men. Opposite, the new power potential of China is visible in the rising dam. With ideological license, Communist China claims its program of irrigation and hydroelectric power, of which San Men Dam is the greatest single work, is the equivalent of 774 Suez Canals or 387 Great Walls.

molded by the combined work of erosion and of man. For hundreds of miles there is hardly a patch of level land that is a natural occurrence, hardly a patch that has not been painfully leveled by generations of farmers in the endless struggle between them and a climate that erodes the land from under their feet. The whole country is terraced on crumbling gradients of yellow loess soil, each slip of a field curbed with a mud wall, in early summer lightly green with corn or millet, hand-sown in hand-plowed ground, which will later be hand-reaped as it has been since the days of earliest cultivation. Embedded in the walls of those terraces are the villages of the farmers, mere rows of caves dug into compact earth.

In the distance there are glimpses of the river flowing placidly enough between the hills, so that it is a shock to turn a bend in the road and arrive at the gorge itself. The soil suddenly disappears and bare rock thrusts up, cleft by the river racing past several hundred feet below.

On my first visit, in the summer of 1957, work on the dam, which was to straddle the two islands in the river, had hardly begun to nibble at the contours of this remarkable scene. The spring spate had gone down, but the river—rich, yellow, and thick as soup with its heavy silt content—still roared through the San Men, or Three Gates, formed by the two islands. It was through this gorge that every boat had

TEXT CONTINUED ON PAGE 11

TEXT CONTINUED FROM PAGE 7

to pass, hauled against the current by its crew, who disembarked and strained on ropes as they stumbled along the catwalks cut into the sides of the cliffs. The deep grooves worn in the rock by the ropes were still there, as were the pious inscriptions ranging in time over a thousand years (page 7). A folk song dating possibly as early as the T'ang Dynasty (A.D. 618–906) described the boatmen's struggle:

The Gate of Ghosts is very dark, a hundred boat-poles deep:
The Gate of Man so narrow that its sides exact their cruel
*   sacrifice.*
The boatmen cry out till their mouths bleed;
Their lives at any moment may float away like feathers.

On a height overlooking the gorge stands a ruined temple dedicated to the legendary Hsia emperor, Yü. There, in former times, a colony of monks fattened on the cash offered by hopeful boatmen about to attempt a passage through the Gate of Man. The names given to the other two channels—Gate of Gods and Gate of Ghosts—indicate local assessment of the hazards of any attempts to pass through them. The temple of Yü is a building of the Ming Dynasty (A.D. 1368–1644); the last of many structures on the same site, its doors are guarded by the curly stone lions beloved of the Mings as symbols of power and majesty. On three of its interior walls are murals of great charm representing scenes of the area (page 10); one depicts the Dragon Boat Festival in which all classes of the people went down to the river to make their sacrifice to the River Dragon. The dragon itself—perennial incarnation of semidivine imperial power—is shown rearing above the turbulent water, ponderous and distinctly self-satisfied with its acknowledged omnipotence.

Like the history of other great civilizations, that of China begins in myth supported by the half-understood evidence of neolithic artifacts scattered along the riverbanks. It seems likely that as early as the fifth millennium B.C. there was a slow interchange of techniques—flint-chipping and, later on, pottery-making—along what was to become the Great Silk Route, from the valley of the Yellow River across central Asia to the more advanced civilizations of the Middle East.

Until the current archaeological campaign, the picture of the neolithic cultures of the San Men region was dim and confused. The recent excavation of two major sites—Miao Ti Kuo and San Li, both near San Men—has revealed the pattern of a hard life of farming and hunting, one which, very early, was peculiarly Chinese in some aspects. The people had dwelt in circular or rectangular pits dug into the earth and roofed with low structures of wood, and doubtless—though none have yet been found—in caves similar to those in the modern villages which I visited (pages 6–7).

Systematic digging has revealed the remains of fires, pottery, storage pits, refuse dumps, burials containing crouched figures, and the regular rows of holes in which roof supports had been set. The stratification of these remains shows the successive habitation of peoples over thousands of years. Characteristically, the excavations reveal three well-marked layers: deepest lies Yangshao; next Lungshan; and, nearest the surface, are traces of the bronze culture of early Eastern Chou times (722–221 B.C.). Until now, most scholars had supposed that the Yangshao and Lungshan cultures (circa 2000 B.C.) had developed independently; the new findings prove conclusively that the Lungshan culture evolved from the Yangshao. This fact is of central importance to Chinese archaeology. With it, and with the new knowledge of neolithic life, we must in due course reappraise every neolithic Chinese pot in the museums of the world.

Apart from the effective simplicity of the designs on many Yangshao pots, I was fascinated by others of the Lungshan period, on which a lizard, applied in relief, peered over the lip as if about to make a quick raid on the contents. Those lizards are some of the earliest graphic representations from China, and one could hardly suppress the feeling that they looked uncommonly like embryonic dragons. Already, three or four thousand years ago, a pattern of life, as evidenced by its utensils, had become recognizably Chinese.

No less important and exciting than the discoveries at neolithic sites near San Men are other finds dating from the Chou period. This dynastic era, the longest in Chinese history, began in the eleventh century B.C., when the Shang Dynasty (successor to the Hsia) was overcome by the Chou people from the west. They set up their capital near Sian and ruled effectively until 771 B.C.; during this period, known as Western Chou, a common culture was diffused throughout northern China. In 771 the Chou, under attack by barbarian tribes, were forced to move their capital east to Loyang; and during the Eastern Chou period, from the late eighth till the third century B.C., their authority diminished and various independent states contended for supremacy.

The earliest historical records from Eastern Chou times are well documented with names of warring principalities, of kings and noble families and ministers, and with evidence of shifts of power. But as far as geographical details go, their vagueness is comparable to that of Homer describing the location of the city of Troy; hence the basic importance of the recent excavation of the Kuo State Cemetery at Shang Ts'un Ling, very near San Men.

There are 234 tombs in the Kuo cemetery, and three chariot pits. The burials all display a consistent pattern: two slit jade rings called *chüeh* at the ears of the body, neck-

TEXT CONTINUED ON PAGE 124

Opposite: A mural depicting life in a typical Yellow River village is part of the painted decoration of the temple of the Great Yü which overlooks the site of the San Men Dam. Safe from the waters' path, it is currently being restored.

Overleaf: The terraced fields of wheat, millet, and tobacco stretch away from San Men in waves of sepia and green. The girl surveyor is one of 200,000 workers camping at San Men; their efforts are transforming the ancient face of the land.

11

In the Han Palace an artist works on a portrait

THE CHINESE IMPERIAL ART TREASURE

During two decades of war and revolution the

Palace collection made its way from Peking to

the western mountains and finally to Formosa.

Some of its prizes are now coming to America

By JAMES CAHILL

AUTHOR OF "CHINESE PAINTING," PUBLISHED BY SKIRA ART BOOKS

In the early part of June this year, an incomparable group of Chinese art treasures, once owned by the Manchu emperors of China, will be put on exhibition at the National Gallery of Art in Washington, D.C. No more than a few of the pieces have been shown previously outside China, and some have never been on public display anywhere. The exhibition, which will travel later to New York, Boston, Chicago, and San Francisco, will be made up of more than two hundred objects in a variety of materials: porcelain, jade, bronze, ivory, lacquer, and others. But the core of it, and the part that should arouse in many art enthusiasts the rare excitement of a major discovery, will be the paintings, more than one hundred of the greatest that have survived, a selection that all the United States museums together could not match.

What will be included in the exhibition is only a tiny fraction of the vast assemblage known as the Palace Museum Collection. It was brought together two centuries ago by an aesthetic emperor, Kao-tsung, who gave to his sixty-year reign (1736–1796) the auspicious title Ch'ien-lung, or "Celestial Prosperity." His aim was to gather in the palace at Peking most of the famous early paintings surviving in his time, those known to the Chinese connoisseurs as *ming-chi*, or "notable relics." His success seems astounding, until one learns of his methods: collectors were persuaded to offer their prized scrolls as "gifts," and the leading connoisseur of the age, one story has it, was deliberately driven to financial ruin and forced to sell his treasures so that they could be added to the imperial hoard. As new pieces were acquired, careful descriptions of them were prepared by a staff of court connoisseurs for insertion in the emperor's catalogue, and the imperial seals were impressed on them in accordance with the practice of Chinese collectors. (Seals of Kao-tsung and of some earlier owners are visible, as square or rectangular designs in red, on several of the paintings reproduced here.)

The fruits of Kao-tsung's acquisitiveness were passed down, more or less intact, by the later Manchu rulers to the last of the line, P'u-i. This ill-fated "boy emperor," less scrupulous than his ancestors in preserving the collection, gave away or otherwise disposed of many of the best pieces. The paintings thus lost are now scattered among museums and private owners throughout the world. What remained was eventually declared the property of the Chinese Republic and installed in 1925 as a public collection in the Palace Museum in Peking.

The history of the museum proper is short: it came to an end in 1933 when the important objects in it—some sixty thousand pieces, including several thousand paintings—were packed in wooden crates and shipped out of Peking to escape the Japanese invasion. They were moved first to Shanghai by sea; then, three years later, to Nanking by rail; and finally, in 1937, far inland to Szechwan Province by whatever means of transport were available under wartime conditions: steamboats for the perilous trip up the Yangtze River, trucks along the steep mountain roads, pack mules or the backs of coolies when there was no passable road. On several occasions, buildings that had served as temporary storage for the crates were destroyed by bombing within weeks, or even days, after they were removed. Surely no art collection of comparable importance has ever traveled so far or undergone such hardships and dangers. Miraculously, very little was lost. After the war ended in 1945, the crates were returned to Nanking. By 1949 they were again on the move, this time to Formosa, following the Nationalist government into exile from the Communist-dominated mainland. They have remained there to the present, stored near Taichung in the central part of the island.

From the very immensity of the collection one might expect that all periods and important schools of painting would be well represented, but they are not. The Ch'ien-lung Emperor was aristocratically orthodox in his tastes. He agreed with his imperial predecessors of the Sung Dynasty (tenth to thirteenth centuries) in admiring the elegant productions of their court academies and evidently had no liking for the rough, spontaneous styles practiced by the Ch'an (Zen) Buddhist monks in the same period. For the later dynasties he accepted the judgments of conservative critics, collected the masters with most prestige, and ignored the startlingly avant-garde creations of the seventeenth- and eighteenth-century individualists. Such gaps in the emperor's taste will be reflected in the exhibition; some kinds of Chinese painting that have lately begun to dazzle Western viewers with their boldness will not be seen in it. Its strength will lie rather in a wealth of what we would call "old masters," paintings that the Chinese themselves have held in highest regard over the centuries.

Landscapes will outnumber pictures of all other subjects, as they should; when we think of Chinese painting, we think first of landscape, which has been the dominant theme for about a millennium. In the earlier periods, however, the favorite subjects dealt with man, his activities and his creations: portraits, historical scenes, illustrations to literature. icons for the Buddhist or Taoist religions. Court artists recorded the quiet occupations of palace ladies or the pleasures of noblemen. A painting attributed to the tenth-century master Chao Yen, from which a detail is reproduced on the cover of this issue, belongs to that genre. But other painters even earlier had begun to portray a world in which man's place was less central and less secure. In the famous *Emperor Ming-huang's Journey to Shu,* probably a close copy of an eighth-century picture, the ostensible theme is the flight into exile of the unfortunate emperor; but this theme is almost obscured by its setting. Ming-huang, whose infatuation with his beautiful concubine Yang Kuei-fei led to his fall from power, is depicted, with his entourage, on a small scale in a lower corner. The artist is plainly more interested in the mountainous terrain itself, the mists flowing among jutting crags, the carefully distinguished varieties of bushes and trees.

As both these pictures illustrate, early Chinese painters delighted in color and decorative detail, adding washes and bright spots of pigment to their fine-line drawing. By the eleventh century, landscapists had renounced these charms, along with their loyalty to specifically human concerns, in pursuit of something more austere and more profound. The supreme achievement of that age and in the opinion of many experts, the greatest surviving Chinese landscape, Fan K'uan's *Traveling Among Streams and Mountains* is executed almost entirely in ink monochrome and has no anecdotal content at all. It is a monumental portrait of a huge rock bluff, which rises sheer from the valley floor and is topped by scrubby vegetation. A waterfall drops down a dark cleft, disappearing in mist at the base. A Buddhist temple nearly hidden among the trees, two travelers driving a train of mules, and a bridge across the stream are the only elements of human intrusion in this imposing vision of the grandeur of nature.

The value of such pictures as these, the Chinese writers maintained, lay in their power of making the observer feel as though he were personally present, gazing at the scene itself instead of at a painting of it. The artist set forth the world very much as he saw it, adding little of obvious comment, only affirming in pictorial terms his deep conviction of a vast but intelligible order behind all its bewildering surface. This relatively objective approach was applied as well to nature close at hand, to pictures of birds, plants, and animals, for example in another masterwork of the eleventh century, the *Hare and Jays* of Ts'ui Po. The season is early winter, the scene a bleak slope from which grow brittle grasses, bamboo,

TEXT CONTINUED ON PAGE 25

A PORTFOLIO OF

CHINESE MASTERPIECES

REPRODUCED BY

ALBERT SKIRA

The paintings which appear on the following eight pages are a sampling of the treasures in the Palace Museum Collection. They were photographed on Formosa for Albert Skira, the Swiss art publisher, and reproduced on his press at Lausanne.

M. Skira, whose books of European painting have set a high standard of art reproduction, has included these paintings, with thirty-two others from the Formosan trove, in a book entitled *Chinese Painting,* the first in a series called "Treasures of Asia." Most of the same paintings will be in the showing of the Palace Museum Collection at the National Gallery in Washington next June.

The photographing of these paintings was personally supervised on Formosa by James Cahill, Associate Curator of Chinese Art at the Freer Gallery in Washington, who is the author of the Skira book as well as of HORIZON's article. Of this undertaking Dr. Cahill writes:

"The village of Pei-kou lies about seven miles outside Taichung in central Formosa, just off the main road leading eastward into the mountains. That road, in mid-August 1959, little more than a week after disastrous floods, was pitted with mud holes and filled in with coarse gravel where parts of it had washed away. Moving carefully along it, fording the river where a bridge was out, were trucks and jeeps, oxcarts, farmers on foot, and a few uncomfortable bicyclists, one of whom was myself. My objective, the Palace Museum Collection, was housed in a cluster of gray concrete buildings at Pei-kou.

"The Chinese committee in charge of the collection, headed by Mr. K'ung Te-ch'eng, direct descendant of Confucius in the seventy-seventh generation, had granted us permission to make fifty color photographs. Since very few of the paintings in the collection had ever been reproduced in color and some not at all, this was a rare privilege. Choosing the fifty out of several thousands required more than a month of steady viewing; I commuted daily from Taichung, though not always by bicycle. Among the dozens of paintings seen every day there were always surprises, totally unknown works of the highest quality.

"The photography was done by Mr. Henry Beville of the National Gallery of Art, who accompanied me on the trip. The paintings, on centuries-old paper and silk, had to be unrolled carefully and handled with extreme caution. Working in a small frame building, in a temperature raised by floodlights even above that of the Formosan summer, Mr. Beville produced a set of superb transparencies that captured all the subtleties of the originals."

The plates for HORIZON's portfolio, as well for the book, engraved in Switzerland and were printed by a process specially developed by M. Skira to convey the mat texture of Oriental paintings on silk.

Ts'ui Po: *Hare and Jays*. Dated 1061. Hanging scroll (cropped
at the bottom). Width: 40¾ inches. Ink and colors on silk.

Anonymous, eleventh-century copy of an eighth-century
composition (?): *The Emperor Ming-huang's Journey to
Shu*. Detail from a hanging scroll. Ink and colors on silk.

Fan K'uan, early eleventh century: *Traveling Among
Streams and Mountains*. Hanging scroll. Height: 61¼
inches. Width: 29¼ inches. Ink and light colors on silk.

Anonymous, late twelfth century (misleading attribution to Chao Po-chü):
The Han Palace. Album leaf. Width: 9¾ inches. Ink and colors on silk.

Li Sung: *The Knick-knack Peddler*. Dated 1210. Album leaf.
Height: 10¼ inches. Width: 10¾ inches. Ink and colors on silk.

Ma Lin: *Listening to the Wind in the Pines*. Seal with the date 1246. Hanging scroll (cropped at top and bottom). Width: 43½ inches. Ink and colors on silk.

Attributed to Chao Kan, tenth century: *A River Journey at First Snow-fall*. Section of a handscroll. Height: 10¼ inches. Ink and colors on silk.

Pien Wen-chin: *The Three Friends and Hundred Birds*. Dated
1413. Detail from a hanging scroll. Ink and colors on silk.

TEXT CONTINUED FROM PAGE 16

and a gnarled tree. A moment in the lives of three wild creatures, a pair of angry jays and an unwelcome rabbit, is captured with a naturalness and absence of artifice that set the painting far apart from those later prettified bird-and-flower designs so much imitated in European *chinoiserie.*

In painting of the twelfth and thirteenth centuries the relations between man and his natural environment took another turn, in the direction of an increased intimacy, and the figures inhabiting Chinese landscapes found themselves in more congenial, less awesome surroundings. This altering of attitude is reflected in two paintings of the tenth and thirteenth centuries, the first attributed to Chao Kan, the second signed by Ma Lin. Both were academy artists and superb technicians, but they differ radically in the ways they present their subjects, and the difference is not to be accounted for entirely by the contrasting character of the subjects themselves. Chao's humble fishermen cower in a shelter of matted reeds, which gives them little protection from the cruel wind. Farther back, a boat carrying travelers is poled by two shivering boatmen. Man's chief concern here is survival in an antagonistic universe; for him to indulge in aesthetic contemplation of the scenery would be unthinkable. Ma Lin's sensitive and elegant scholar, on the other hand, is doing just that, sitting in a tense pose, consciously attuning his mind to the sound of the wind in the pines. The world around him, unnaturally tidy, looks as though it had been fashioned for his pleasure.

Paintings in this milder mode, produced by academy artists during the second half of the Sung Dynasty, are the best known of all Chinese paintings in the Occident, and will very likely hold their popularity in the coming exhibition, in which they are well represented. No one, however unacquainted with things Oriental, can remain immune to the warmth of their mood, the charm of their subjects, the brilliance of their technique. Especially attractive are the meticulously painted miniatures, in the forms of album leaves and fan paintings. The latter were originally mounted on flat fans and later removed to albums for better preservation. Their identifying oval shape may be seen in the two reproduced here. The first, titled *The Han Palace,* represents the evening of the Double Seven, the autumn festival. Palace ladies pass in stately procession before a lamplit hall on their way through a rock tunnel to the tower in the upper left, from which they will view the autumn moon. The quiet mood of twilight pervades the picture. The painter of the other, Li Sung, ventured forth from the palace to find his subject on a country road. A peddler of toys and knick-knacks has set down his load and turns to deliver a sales talk to his customers, four excited little boys who tug their mother toward him. A baby suckling at her breast reaches out to make its choice. The drawing is fantastically fine, and the artist, justifiably proud of it, has saved his audience the trouble of counting the individual objects in the peddler's pack by writing "Five Hundred Articles" on the trunk of the willow in characters so small they can barely be read.

With the fall of the Sung Dynasty in the late thirteenth century, the imperial academy went out of existence, and the kinds of painting perfected within it fell into decline. The dominant movements in later centuries aimed at very different ends and made use of fundamentally different styles. The strongest current was that known as *wen-jen hua,* or "literati painting," done by scholar-amateurs rather than by professionals. Technical finish gave way to a disregard for skill that sometimes reached the point of deliberate gaucherie, and the most appealing qualities of academy painting were sacrificed in favor of a cool, more intellectual approach. There was, however, a short-lived revival of the academic tradition at the beginning of the Ming Dynasty in the late fourteenth and early fifteenth centuries. Several emperors of that period supported artists in their courts, in what seems to have been a conscious attempt to recapture the brilliance of Sung painting. How far they succeeded can be seen in the work of one of these court artists, Pien Wen-chin, an early fifteenth-century master of bird-and-flower themes. His *Three Friends and Hundred Birds* uses the so-called "three friends of the cold winter," the pine, bamboo, and flowering plum, as perches for a colorful throng such as the most optimistic bird watcher could scarcely hope to encounter. Much of the old charm is there, but much else has been lost, including the sympathetic understanding of the birds themselves that makes a masterwork of the Ts'ui Po picture.

These few examples only begin to suggest the diversity of styles and subjects to be represented among the paintings in the coming exhibition. Everyone will have his particular favorites, and no one is likely to admire them all. There are varieties of Chinese painting toward which one warms only slowly, just as there are in Western art. But the exhibition as a whole will reveal Chinese painting in its full richness to a great many people and establish it for them in the high position it merits within world art. And perhaps the Emperor Kao-tsung, however undemocratic his purpose may have been, deserves in the end some gratitude for that.

One of the theater's most eminent directors considers the quality of greatness

on the stage, recalling great players in great plays which "open the windows

of the imagination in the way that the theater uniquely can but seldom does"

HENRY GROSSMAN

Guthrie at rehearsal

GREATNESS
IN THE THEATER

By TYRONE GUTHRIE

Theatrical art is writ on water. Its greatest charm is that it is evanescent. Ideas expressed in literature, sculpture, or painting are set down in a material form and are thus guaranteed survival until the material is destroyed. Theatrical art has no material survival. At the end of even the greatest performance, what is left? Nothing but some dingy scenery and properties, a rumpled dress, a hat, a sword, some worthless jewels, and—a legend. The legend will not last long; but for a while and for a few it is a joy, a stimulus, a life-enriching thing, not wholly unworthy to be considered great.

Another aspect of theatrical greatness is that it seems always to exist in the past: I have noticed that "great acting" is seldom going on right now—it usually occurred at least twenty years ago; and "great plays" are by authors who are

dead, or at any rate, in the last stages of senescence. They acquire greatness when those who saw them in their impressionable youth have reached an age when only the most golden memories survive and when their verdict carries authority.

In my youth, in Britain, the legendary figures of the stage were Duse and Bernhardt and, of course, our own Henry Irving and Ellen Terry. But even their legends were eclipsed by those of the great operatic stars—Melba, the De Reszke brothers, Mary Garden, Chaliapin, Tamagno, Caruso—for these were days when Grand Opera was still supremely grand. Opera was the occasion for a display of diamonds, bouquets of orchids, tuberoses, and stephanotis, all of which got mixed, in the memories of aunts and grandparents, with cadenzas and finales and carriages and pairs and trios and quartets and linkmen and footmen and the Nun's Chorus—a glorious, glamourous jumble, but unquestionably "great."

At that time of my life I accepted these legends readily enough. I was prepared to believe that to have seen Sir Henry Irving's Richelieu was a greater theatrical experience than I should ever undergo; but for my own part I was inclined to be quite satisfied with the lesser "greatness" of Sir Gerald du Maurier, the Abbey Theatre (still in its heyday), Sybil Thorndike, and other gods and goddesses of the twenties. Also, by this time we were in the era of silent movie stars. Is it because I was so much younger, or was it the fact that they were silent and consequently more mysterious, more removed from ordinary humanity, which made them seem "greater" than their audible successors? Pauline Frederick, as I remember her, was more sweepingly tragédienne than the film stars of today; and I do not think that any of the present male stars, except Charles Laughton, have come up to the stature of Emil Jannings. I think that most people, not just veterans of my epoch, would agree that Chaplin was greater then than now, greater when he was still satisfied to be a pathetic little mime and when the limitations of his medium precluded all too explicit Messages about Grave Issues. Legendary figures, when encountered, do not always live up to their legendary reputations, especially when the hand of the years, so flattering to the legend, has fallen heavily upon the original.

It was in 1915, I think, that I saw Sarah Bernhardt, then in her late seventies. She was the principal act on the bill of one of London's music halls, and her "turn" was the recitation of *Les Cathédrales,* a piece which had been specially written for her because her right leg had recently been amputated and she could no longer walk, but lay propped up on a sort of bier. My recollection of the piece is vague; I think she impersonated Strasbourg Cathedral and chanted about the maimed and desecrated shrines of war-torn France. It should have been extremely impressive and poignant, but it was not. It was only sad. The *voix d'or* was hoarse and feeble; the fires which once had blazed now barely glowed. I wished I had not been there.

A few years later Melba gave a recital at Oxford. She was in her late sixties, a splendidly strong and forcible person but not a gracious or attractive performer. She ran through an exacting program of classical excerpts and popular ballads with unsmiling efficiency, using the remnants of her voice with extraordinary skill. It was a demonstration of vocal technique and disciplined will power, but as an artist wooing an audience—one predominantly young, ardent, and wishful to adore—she was a disappointment. That this formidable battle-ax still sang with the limpid, apparently effortless sweetness of a blackbird seemed only strange and eerie.

As time went on I accumulated recollections that had for me legendary proportions, but remember that I do not claim for them objective greatness. They were great to me *then*; they glow more brightly, not less, with the passing years, but if I had the same experiences now that I have more discrimination and less energy, perhaps some of them would not seem great at all. Who knows?

In the winter of 1920–21 two friends from Oxford and I spent a week in Dresden. We went to the opera every night. It was an eye opener and an ear opener as well, for it was a very good period at Dresden. The intendant was Tauber, whose son Richard was destined to achieve world popularity a little later as a tenor in light opera. The cast was illustrious, the repertoire varied and interesting, and the productions lavish and carefully rehearsed.

The high spot of the week was *Der Rosenkavalier.* In those days the score seemed daringly modern, and the décor was elegant. The Marschallin was Elisabeth Schumann; Baron Ochs, whose name I forget, was funny and pitiful as well and had the sort of voice you might expect to hear if an enormous oak tree were miraculously able to sing. The opera has the great advantage of ending gloriously: the trio of women's voices soar up and up, in harmonies which then seemed deliciously, lushly exotic. I came out of the theater in a trance of delight, which has lasted, intermittently but keenly, for forty years. The memory of this production is still a delight, though now *Der Rosenkavalier* seems neither modern nor amusing—just a heavy, indigestible, Germanic sweetmeat.

Also in the early twenties, but in London, I made my first contact with ballet—the Diaghilev company. Ballet was not as yet popular; it was still considered avant-garde. The company appeared at the London Colosseum and did a twenty-minute "turn" in the vaudeville program. The first ballet that I saw was *The Good-Humoured Ladies,* which was comedic, not romantic, and had a charming score arranged from Scarlatti. Lopokova, at her best, danced the leading role, and the whole thing was a revelation in its complete absence of heavy, matter-of-fact realism. Later I saw *Carnaval* and *Scheherezade* with décors by Bakst. They were still magical, but I preferred the merriment of *The Good-Humoured Ladies* to the more romantic works. A year or two later I encountered *Les Sylphides,* with Fokine's choreography to a score arranged from Chopin. Has anyone since made a more expressive and simple choreography or one which, without story or literal meaning, has so much to say?

In the middle 1920's Diaghilev, encouraged by the success of his earlier seasons, took a huge London theater and mounted a three-hour ballet, which I think was called *Aurora's Wedding.* A huge orchestra played a huge score by Tchaikovsky; a glittering cast danced superlatively; the scenery was sumptuous and in the best rococo taste—and the whole evening was a pretentious bore. I have not yet seen a full-length ballet which has managed to sustain interest, and even by the end of a program of well-diversified short ballets I begin to weary of elegant gymnastics and the rather limited vocabulary of the dance and to long for someone neither beautiful nor exotic, but sensible, to come and *say* something pithy and terse and even, possibly, vulgar.* It

*For an answer to this complaint see the interview with George Balanchine, especially the paragraphs on page 46.—ED.

makes me wonder whether ballet can ever be anything by itself. Perhaps it can. But in my experience a whole evening of ballet is like having nothing but Charlotte Russe for dinner, topped off, maybe, by a very tiny Angel-on-Horseback.

This is not to deny that ballet, especially the Diaghilev ballet, has had a great influence upon the taste of two generations, especially in visual matters. In 1909 Bakst struck Western Europe like a stone flung into a pond. The ripples extended and extended, slowly but ever widening; by the middle twenties all the department stores were offering curtains, wallpaper, and summer frocks unblushingly derived from the designs of Bakst and others of Diaghilev's Russian artists. Later Diaghilev began choosing his designers in France—Picasso, Derain, Matisse, De Chirico, and so on. But fine as many of the later Diaghilev productions were, none of them had the same influence upon popular taste as those of his earlier Russian period.

Even today the curtains which flutter damply in Presbyterian manses in the Scottish Highlands, the aprons which cover the ample fronts of housewives in North Dakota are—little though their owners may know it—the last ripples from the stone which Diaghilev and his decorators flung into the pond of human consciousness.

For the public, at least, I suppose that it is the work of the actors, rather than that of the playwright, which stamps an evening in the theater as "great." Over the last forty years I have seen most of the finest performers in the English-speaking theater. To compare one with another is like comparing chalk with cheese. The classics are the only measuring rod by which the stature of an actor or a director can be compared. How can you say whether A in a classical tragedy is greater than B in a farce or C in a naturalistic portrayal of ordinary middle-class humanity? Such comparisons are made, but with rare exceptions it is the personalities rather than the art and skill of the artists which are the point of comparison. Criticism degenerates into gossip. But it *is* possible, and it is a matter of great interest and of serious critical value to compare the Hamlets, let us say, of Barrymore, Gielgud, Olivier, Maurice Evans, Christopher Plummer, and the host of others who from time to time attempt the part and risk the comparison. Rather than embark on so studied an effort here, I shall only try to tell why some performances I have seen—and those *not* necessarily comparable—have left so great an impression.

Of many Hamlets, Gielgud was the greatest. I have seen him in three productions of *Hamlet*: the first at the Old Vic in 1930, when he was little more than a student; the second in the West End of London three or four years later; the third, again in London, about ten years after that. I think that the second was the best. Already he had lost (or was it not he but I?) a little of the boyish eagerness and earnestness which made his first, very young Hamlet such a poignant experience. Already the tone of the voice, the cadence of a phrase, the turn of the head, the stance, the walk were fa-

When Tyrone Guthrie saw Sarah Bernhardt (1844–1923) in 1915, he expected to find the experience poignant: "It was only sad."

PHOTOGRAPHS CULVER PICTURES INC.

The author recalls Nellie Melba (1861–1931) in 1918 as a "formidable battle-ax," her singing still "apparently effortless."

miliar; were, through use, becoming a little mannered. The scenes between Hamlet and his mother were still remarkable, but they were less touching, and perhaps less true, now that the son was no longer a young beginner but a confident and successful star. On the other hand, the scenes with the Ghost and with Claudius had gained enormously in power and understanding. No other actor of our day has conveyed so well the mixture of fear and awe of the Ghost with the touching affection of a son for a recently dead father. It was a statement about the relation of all sons to all fathers in uniquely vivid terms. It was great acting, commenting in a way which neither sculpture, painting, literature, music, nor philosophy can achieve.

Further, of all contemporary actors Gielgud is to my mind the finest rhetorician. He is not the greatest impersonator; his range is not very wide nor his sympathy very catholic, but he commands a magnificently expressive music of speech. The voice is a good one but not better than many; technically he has never mastered a tendency toward strangulation and loss of resonance in the upper register and weakness in the lower. But his inflections are uniquely musical, varied, and expressive; his contrasts of tempo and rhythm, his use of staccato and legato, of vocal color—all these are masterly.

Finally—and this is greatly valuable in Hamlet though occasionally in other parts obtrusive and malapropos—Gielgud is of all actors the most royal. By stance and gesture, by the attitudes of gracious friendliness, wit, displeasure, or rage, he can suggest without effort or exaggeration that he is a prince among subjects. This is the more striking and endearing because off the stage he is a simple, unassertive man, easily disconcerted and made shy, so that it is sometimes hard to appreciate in him the staunchness and tenacity which, as well as talent, are needed to bring an actor to the top of his profession and keep him there.

Another great classical performance was that of Laurence Olivier as Richard III. (I refer to the Old Vic Company's production at the New Theatre in London in 1944–45. The subsequent film was but a poor pale shadow of the original.) Olivier is less of a rhetorician than Gielgud but more of an actor. His range is immense: every characterization is different—he looks different, sounds different, moves differently—but every characterization is suffused with humor. I have seen him in dozens of parts and enjoyed him in all, although I have not agreed with some of the interpretations. For instance, in the film, his Hamlet seemed to me the portrait of a Nazi gauleiter rather than that of a delicate and tender prince; his Lear, for the Old Vic in 1946–47, had moments of extraordinary imagination but was sentimental rather than monumental. It was as though King Lear had been rewritten by Dickens; one almost expected Cordelia to call him "Daddy." But in *Richard III* the intention was as clear as it was forcible; it was, as I believe Shakespeare intended, a monstrous and gloriously amusing caricature, a gargoyle. The make-up—long sharp nose, long lank black

N. Y. PUB. LIB. DANCE COLLECTION

In the 1920's Guthrie encountered ballet—the Diaghilev company. He found Scheherezade *"magical," especially its costumes and décor by Bakst, which "struck Western Europe like a stone flung into a pond." But he preferred the merriment of* The Good-Humoured Ladies.

hair, thin mouth, and darting beady eyes—was fantastic but, in the context, credible. He was attractive enough to lend credence to the strange love scene with Lady Anne; he presented power-lust with really terrifying force but always in the key of caricature; the haunted dreams of the final sequence were a crescendo of thrilling nervous tension, culminating in a death at once horrible and ignominious but performed with a perverted grandeur. The best moments of all were when Richard played cat and mouse with the doomed little Princes on their way to the Tower. He was the distilled essence of Wicked Uncle, a creature straight out of legend or dream, amusing while uncomfortably fearsome.

But with Olivier it is not one part which makes him great: it is the sum of his gallery of parts. And it is in this respect that the British theater, in spite of a superficial decadence, is still better organized than the American. Over the past twenty or thirty years the American theater has produced many splendid talents, but the circumstances of professional life have forced them into narrow channels. No American actor has been able, as has Olivier, to range from Oedipus, Romeo, Hamlet, Lear, Antony, Titus Andronicus, or Richard III to Justice Shallow, Toby Belch, Mr. Puff, Harry Rich (the venal and tormented vaudevillian who is *The Entertainer* of John Osborne), or the pathetically bored and vapid young fellow in Terence Rattigan's *Sleeping Prince*. Even if one does not always agree with the interpretation, one cannot fail to thrill to the extraordinary verve, intelli-

gence, and humor that mark the style of the interpreter.

Rather a similar art is that of Sybil Thorndike. She, like Olivier, can and will take a shot at anything. The energy and the technique are terrific. As with Olivier, you may not always agree with the interpretation, but you must always feel that you are in the presence of a being in whom, and through whom, life flows with the force of a great, rushing wind. Like Olivier, she excels in portraits larger than life-sized, tragic and grotesque. Her Medea was, I think, the most exciting performance I have ever seen. It was an exhibition of the beastlike, self-destructive savagery which underlies the varnished surface of human existence. Dame Sybil Thorndike is not a tall woman, but such was the force of this performance that she seemed, during its climax of rage and despair, literally to grow to towering, superhuman stature.

Edith Evans has shared with Sybil Thorndike a paramount position among the serious actresses of the British theater. But whereas Thorndike has excelled in performances which call for grotesque frenzy, madness, violence, and caricature, Evans has been at her best in the realm of high comedy—where artifice reveals nature, where sophisticated simulation reveals simple truth.

The finest performance which I have seen her give was as Rosalind in the Old Vic production of *As You Like It* in 1937. She was nearer fifty than forty at the time—rather old, you may think, for Rosalind. Indeed, for the first five or six minutes of the performance it did seem rather effron-

Of many Hamlets that he has seen, Guthrie considers Sir John Gielgud to be the greatest, "the finest rhetorician . . . the most royal."

Guthrie notes of Sir Laurence Olivier, "every characterization is different"; as Richard III he was "the distilled essence of Wicked Uncle."

tery for this big, middle-aged woman to get up and masquerade as a young girl, dressed as a boy and wildly in love with an Orlando (Michael Redgrave, then in his twenties) young enough to be her son. But then the magic of great acting swept aside all reservations. The performance was more, not less, moving, because it was a comment upon young love and young girlhood enriched by the wisdom, sympathy, and technical brilliance of a mature actress. It was a feast of spoken music, a revelation of how Shakespearian verse, when wonderfully spoken, gilds the meaning of words and opens the windows of the imagination in the way that the theater uniquely can but seldom does.

If most of my memories of great acting derive from the British theater rather than the American, it is for two reasons. First, I did not see any great American acting until I was too old to be easily swept away; second, the American theater of today, with its insistence upon naturalism and its timid avoidance of what might possibly be considered "ham." does not encourage great acting. There is no room for great acting in little plays; as a mixed-up kid you can be poignant, you can show great promise, but you cannot be great. It is unfortunate that the American theater for some years has been obsessed with the problems of mixed-up kids—albeit often kids of forty-seven.

I do, however, include in my gallery of great memories two American performances: Laurette Taylor in *The Glass Menagerie* and the joint performance, so articulated that it

cannot be taken apart and considered as anything but a single unit, of the Lunts in *The Guardsman.*

The Glass Menagerie, although I think it a masterpiece, is a small masterpiece, and Eddie Dowling's direction was unhelpfully and feebly vague. But Laurette Taylor's performance was a lesson in how great acting, even within a small and realistic framework, can still be great. It was a miniature painted with such insight and, at the same time, such power that it had the force of a great portrait. Only a mature and enormously accomplished artist can do this; only the wisdom and sympathy of maturity could show, as Laurette Taylor showed, the element of helpless childishness in human maturity, the littleness of mankind in the complex jungle of a civilization which we pretend to control.

The Guardsman in less brilliant hands than those of Alfred Lunt and Lynn Fontanne could easily seem rather silly and vulgar. What one saw was a consummate piece of artifice; it was the sort of exquisite but tiny workmanship which goes into the making of jewelry or a watch. I suppose it is idle to regret that the great talent, the unexcelled technique and unique partnership of these two players has been used to make so many beautiful but immemorable toys.

I remember Thornton Wilder saying in quite another context what a pity it was that Queen Victoria had not been a patroness of the theater. Then Dickens, a thwarted man of the theater, would have written for the stage. We can be grateful for *David Copperfield, The Pickwick Papers,* or

As Rosalind in the Old Vic's As You Like It, *Dame Edith Evans's "comment upon young love was enriched by the wisdom" of maturity.*

In Glass Menagerie *Laurette Taylor painted a miniature "with such insight . . . such power that it had the force of a great portrait."*

31

Great Expectations; but Wilder thought, and I agree, that masterpieces though they be, they would have been still greater had they been written as plays rather than as novels. Likewise, what a pity it is that the American theater has found no Molière or Congreve for the Lunts to interpret.

So far I have been recalling the actors who have provided me with great memories. I have been impressed by great directors, too. First was Max Reinhardt, whose *Jedermann* I viewed at Salzburg. *Jedermann* is not a great play, but Reinhardt made it seem so. The set was the steps of the cathedral; its backdrop was the cathedral's elaborate baroque façade, and in the foreground was spread an enormous banquet table of which I recall no details except a profusion of fruit and flowers—dahlias in scarlet, crimson, yellow, and purple. The whole production was keyed up to the size of the stage. The German language lends itself to boomy, majestic acting, and the company, magnificently led by Alexander Moissi, maintained a huge scale of declamation, supported by an emotion of similar depth and breadth without which the booming speech would have become mere empty noise.

In sharp contrast I remember Harold Clurman's direction of the Group Theater in Odets's *Golden Boy.* I saw the Group in London, and I have heard that their American production of the play was even better. But what we saw was superb—an orchestrated ensemble in which each player, while part of the strictly disciplined whole, still seemed a virtuoso in his own right—from Luther Adler as the Golden

Boy down to the smallest small-part player on the fringe.

The Group seemed at the time (the late thirties) to be a really modern theater; dealing in a contemporary manner with current issues, they were serious but not ponderous, and they revealed the development, to a higher power, of a sort of modern comedy which in London had lost its way among the teacups. It was this production of *Golden Boy* which made me determine, someday and somehow, to make myself a part of the American theater, which I, like so many others in Britain and indeed all over the world, had supposed to be created in the image which America presents to the world—the Hollywood image.

Finally, I recall the greatest production I have yet seen. It had been made in Moscow in the early 1920's. I saw it in London a decade later. This was a production by Vakhtangov for the Jewish company known as Habima, which means in Hebrew "The Stage."

In 1917, during the early turmoils of the revolution, a small group of Jewish aspirants in Moscow determined to form a company and present a repertoire of Jewish plays. They sought the assistance of Konstantin Stanislavsky, the director of the Moscow Art Theatre. He was impressed with their seriousness and zeal and recommended that they engage one of his most promising pupils, Eugene Vakhtangov, as their adviser and coach, which they did.

About this time the Jewish poet Bialik published the translation from Yiddish into Hebrew of Ansky's play *The*

N. Y. PUB. LIB. THEATER COLLECTION

Particularly aware of the director's contribution, Guthrie recollects with delight the Max Reinhardt production of Jedermann: *"not a great play, but Reinhardt made it seem so."*

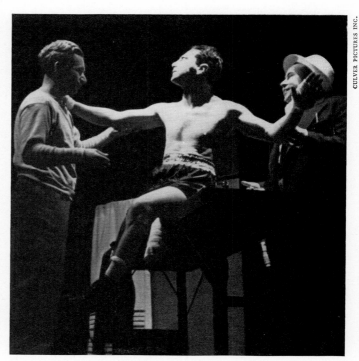

CULVER PICTURES INC.

About Harold Clurman's direction of Golden Boy *for the Group Theater, Guthrie remarks that it was "an orchestrated ensemble in which each player . . . seemed a virtuoso."*

Dybbuk. It is a story of the possession of a young girl by a lost soul. The idea, while romantic and theatrical, is treated with reverence and dignity, and the material appealed to Vakhtangov. He made out of it, working with the inexperienced but gifted young group, something extraordinary.

The scenery was schematic—not much more than some benches, a long table, and a background of white sheets—but the use of false perspective and a steeply raked platform made these simple elements the basis for some astonishing pictorial effects. The speech, make-up, and movement of the actors were highly stylized: speech moved imperceptibly into song and back again; walking changed to dancing and then back to ordinary walking. As with Clurman's production of *Golden Boy,* the discipline of the ensemble did not obscure but rather highlighted the individual talents. I shall never forget the performances of Anna Rovina as the possessed girl and of Jehoshua Bertonov as the Messenger of God.

In its absolute rejection of naturalism, in its concept of drama as ritual, and in its use of liturgical formulas not just as inserted decoration but as the principal means of communication, the production was, of course, far ahead of its time. Even now we are only beginning to explore some of the technical and theoretical ideas which Vakhtangov suggested.

It is a poignant fact that even as he was rehearsing *The Dybbuk,* Vakhtangov, then quite a youngster, was dying of cancer. The actors knew that he was ill and often in pain; they did not know how near he was to the end (he died that year). I have heard this from several members of the original cast: they felt that this production, in a special sense, was the testament of Vakhtangov. They worked on it, and for him, with a special devotion. His work, and theirs, has not been wasted. The production has been given all over the world; scores of thousands have been thrilled and moved by it. It is still, after forty years, the crown of Habima's repertory in Israel, and as was the case with Diaghilev's ballet, the ripples from its original impact in Moscow are still spreading into the most remote and unexpected places.

Perhaps the test of true greatness in the theater is the degree to which a play, a production, or a performance continues to create an impact, a force that makes itself felt across the years. Great works endure in literary form, but a play, locked between the covers of a book, is like a precious mineral hidden in the earth. From time to time down the years, great drama is mined and polished and fashioned into a jewel by gifted interpreters who offer it, glittering and sparkling, to the eye of each generation briefly, even momentarily, but with a brilliance which is memorable and thrilling long after the bright bauble has been cast aside.

The most internationally acclaimed of directors—London's Old Vic, Canada's Stratford Festival, Israel's Habima, numerous Broadway productions—Tyrone Guthrie writes frequently of the theater. His autobiography, A Life in the Theatre, *was published in 1959.*

CULVER PICTURES INC.

To Guthrie the greatest production he has yet seen was that of The Dybbuk *as directed for Habima by Eugene Vakhtangov: "something extraordinary. . . . In its absolute rejection of naturalism, in its concept of drama as ritual . . . the production was far ahead of its time."*

From its breathtaking perch on a Bavarian crag, Ludwig's castle of Neuschwanstein looks down on the glimmering little Alpsee

DREAM CASTLES

bourgeois age in which he lived. But that was only as long as Bavarian patience—and money—held out

EWING KRAININ, COURTESY PAN AMERICAN WORLD AIRWAYS

"They called him the Crazy King! Well, I will tell you something," the guide on the tourist bus confided into a loudspeaker. "The Crazy King was *not crazy at all!*"

We were parked alongside a souvenir-and-postcard stall on the grounds of Schloss Linderhof, the sumptuous hunting lodge built some eighty years ago in the Bavarian Alps by King Ludwig II. Warm May weather had brought out sightseers, including a good many Bavarian peasants, and the atmosphere was festive, almost carnival. Souvenirs and postcards were selling briskly and so, at the outdoor restaurant nearby, were beer and *wurst*.

The guide was a glum and discouraged-looking man, but now that he began to speak of Ludwig, a note of enthusiasm came into his voice. "He was against war, he was against Prussia, and he loved art—so they said he was crazy! He was also very religious—so religious that he could not marry anyone because he was secretly in love with his cousin, the Empress Elizabeth of Austria." Here the guide paused and, with something like royal disdain, looked at the apathetic tourist-faces before him. "Now we get out of the bus and we go through the castle. He hated crowds, the great king. He was a real Bavarian, he liked to go away to the mountains. In Munich they said he was so extravagant he must be crazy—but today the State of Bavaria can afford to keep up its other old castles because of the admission fees at Linderhof, Neuschwanstein, and Herrenchiemsee. So who's crazy? Don't touch anything and don't walk on the parquet."

The Bavarians, who love fairy tales, cherish this one—a potpourri of truth, fantasy, and speculation about King Ludwig. Although the real Ludwig, a stout, unhappy man, died at the age of forty in 1886, shortly after being taken in hand by psychiatrists, a fairy-tale Ludwig still survives: a tall, blue-eyed youth with dark wavy hair, who did exactly what he pleased—which was to build castles. The three strange, resplendent castles he built, each grandly and remotely placed and glittering with riches, are so impractical as to be of use only to a fugitive from reality. Ludwig never intended them to be used in the ordinary sense: he had no queen and no children, never held any state dinners, balls, or receptions, and, since he never invited anyone to spend the night, needed but one bedroom to a castle (two in Herrenchiemsee, the extra one being intended for the mystical convenience of the long-dead Louis XIV of France). Today, all the royal apartments look nearly as pristine as they must have looked

By MARY CABLE   35

One of Ludwig's favorite pastimes, aside from building castles, was to take solitary midnight rides in a golden rococo sleigh. Servants and horses were always en grande tenue—eighteenth-century livery, powdered wigs, blue morocco harness, and blue and white plumes. Ludwig himself sometimes wore an ermine-lined blue velvet robe, sometimes dressed in the style of Louis XIV or XV, and sometimes—presumably in his informal moods, as in this painting by R. Wenig—settled for a large diamond brooch in his hat.

in the 1880's. There are no scratches, no worn carpets, no fragile springs. The rich colors of the draperies—violet, crimson, emerald, sky, or lapis, blue—have scarcely faded. Here and there the fabric is disintegrating, but only from time and the weight of gold embroidery, not from the touch of human fingers. These are enchanted castles, not meant for flesh and blood.

Ludwig does not seem to have had any creative talents himself, and he never sought any training in architecture or design. But he was adept at writing "approved" or "not approved" on the sketches of the many architects and designers who worked for him, and he supervised his castle-building down to the last doorknob, so that the over-all result reflects

Ludwig and no one else. Everywhere are enigmatic clues to his personality: What sort of man, one wonders, would feel that he needed a throne of cast-zinc peacock feathers? Or a couch with mirrors at head and foot, so that he could see himself ad infinitum? Or a golden rococo sleigh drawn by six plumed horses in which to ride by moonlight all alone? A study of Ludwig's life explains some of this; the rest swirls away in a pretty mist of legend and fairy tale—and, perhaps, in the smoke of burned papers and letters.

Why has Ludwig become a hero? We can only guess. Perhaps his countrymen, drilled from childhood in strict discipline and obedience, nourish a secret longing to jump over the moon and are delighted by a king who tried to do so.

PHOTO KEMPTER

Ludwig Friedrich Wilhelm Wittelsbach was born at Nymphenburg Palace, Munich, on August 25, 1845. His grandfather, Ludwig I in the line of Wittelsbach rulers of Bavaria, was then king: pleasure-loving, cultivated, willful, and not of great use to his country except as an importer of opera, art, and elegant manners and as an embellisher of the city of Munich. The baby's father, Crown Prince Maximilian, was a more typical Bavarian: bourgeois in his tastes, conservative, and given to romanticism and flowery sentiment, provided these did not too outrageously conflict with common sense. Maximilian's consort was Marie of Prussia, a woman of not many brains but with normal control of those she had. Years later, it was said in Bavaria that the taint

of insanity that afflicted both Ludwig and his younger brother Otto, who was hopelessly insane from boyhood, came from the Prussians, but the fact was that several Wittelsbachs had been locked away and that Ludwig I himself was a man of such ungoverned passions as to border on the pathological.

When Ludwig I was sixty-two years old, soon after the birth of his grandson, his eye lighted up at the sight of Lola Montez, the redoubtable Spanish dancer from Limerick, Ireland, and she became his acknowledged mistress. Emulating the Bourbon kings of France, whom he dearly loved to emulate, the aging king not only showered his mistress with jewels, money, and titles, but allowed her to hire and fire ministers of state. Unfortunately for Ludwig, the year 1848

37

KEETMAN, COURTESY ROY BERNARD

Herrenchiemsee is the most extravagant of Ludwig's castles —a hyperthyroid version of Versailles with more gilt, more glitter, more chandeliers, and more candelabras than in the original. Its great Hall of Mirrors (at right) is not only more overpoweringly sumptuous than the one at Versailles, but bigger. Not that Ludwig had any use for a room of such size: he spent only a few nights at Herrenchiemsee and never entertained anyone—except, possibly, the ghost of Louis XIV.

was at hand, a bad one for kings; this final nonsense was too much for the Bavarians. Ludwig's cabinet—called, by an indignant populace shouting in the streets, the Lolaministerium—resigned, and the King abdicated. Maximilian thereupon succeeded to the throne, and the infant Ludwig became Crown Prince.

The boy grew up in an environment that was strict, loveless, rigidly formal, and, at the same time, pervaded with rampant romanticism. King Max and Queen Marie bought Hohenschwangau, an old ruined castle in the Bavarian Alps, and set about restoring it to what they perhaps imagined to have been its original state. Because the medieval lords of Schwangau had had a swan on their escutcheon, Maximilian, carried away by the newly awakened Pan-Germanic enthusiasm for Middle High German lore, decided to link the castle

with Lohengrin and ordered enormous murals for the royal apartments showing scenes from the Lohengrin legend. The furniture of the castle was Gothic, most of it pale ash. In his bedroom the King had murals of the love affair of Tasso's Rinaldo and Armida, and the ceiling was covered with stars and orange trees. As for the Queen, she fancied dreamy Oriental landscapes and Turkish knickknacks. Lohengrin's swan was embroidered on the draperies and chair seats, carved on the woodwork, chiseled on the silver serving dishes, painted on the ceilings; and, of course, there were whole flotillas of swans adrift on the beautiful lake, the Schwansee, far below the castle windows. (One day, years later, Ludwig II was to push the swan motif even further by dressing a young man in Lohengrin armor and setting him forth on the lake in a real swan boat.) The royal family was much at-

HERPICH & SON

tached to Hohenschwangau and spent several months of each year there.

From the age of eight, Ludwig had lessons all day long; for some reason, it had been decided that he would learn in five years what Bavarian school children learned in eight, and as he grew older he often studied from half past five in the morning until eight in the evening. The lesson he seems to have learned best was that next to his father he was the most important personage around. His governess one day was dismayed to find that he had stolen a small gaudy purse from a shop near the royal residence at Hohenschwangau. "But why have I done wrong?" he asked. "Why should it be a sin? One day I shall be king of this country, and all that belongs to my subjects belongs to me."

King Max died in 1864, and Ludwig, now eighteen years old, succeeded him. The young King was six-foot-three and strikingly handsome, and the Bavarians, catching one of their first good views of him as he walked through the streets of Munich behind his father's coffin, were delighted with him. They clamored to see him more often, and the more they clamored, the more elusive he became. He feared crowds, disdained persons of common birth, and was happiest when by himself or watching a play or an opera (before long he began to combine these pleasures by having theatrical performances put on for him alone). He had seen *Lohengrin* for the first time when he was fifteen and apparently had jumped to the conclusion that a man who could bring heroes to life must necessarily be a hero, too, for one of his first acts as King was to seek out Richard Wagner—who was hard to find because he was hiding from creditors—and send

Linderhof (below) is the only castle that Ludwig ever completed or that he actually lived in for any length of time. Its interior is rococo pushed as far as it will go, and then some; but it pales beside the unchecked fantasy of a few of the outbuildings—especially the Grotto (right), part Capri and part Venusberg. Here Ludwig swam or rowed beneath the fake stalactites, and though few guests ever saw it, he once brought in his favorite horse to admire the lighting effects.

HANS HUBER—BLACK STAR

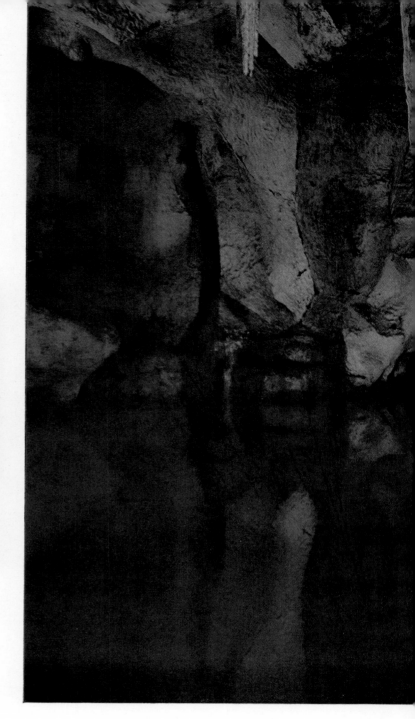

for him, pay his debts, and provide him with a house in Munich, a castle on Lake Starnberg, and a comfortable income.

Ludwig himself does not seem to have been musical: after five years of piano lessons, his tutor had said there was no point in going on, because his Royal Highness the Crown Prince has "neither talent for music nor does he like it. . . ." It was not for music that he idolized Wagner but for the Wagnerian themes, and if the composer had set other stories to music, he would probably never have met the King of Bavaria. Ludwig's mind was drenched in fantasy, and his human relationships were significant to him only insofar as they helped make fantasy seem real. His obsession was to shut out the world of nineteenth-century Germany, where monarchs were bothered by niggling financial ministers,

where a Prussian bully, Count Bismarck, was destroying Bavarian sovereignty, and where (even worse) no one talked in poetry, and rooms were apt to be stuffed with Biedermeier furniture. To Ludwig, a royal Miniver Cheevy, almost any other century looked better.

At first, he was graciously willing to take his people along with him on his magic carpet: one of his first big projects was a rococo opera house, to be built especially for the première of the complete *Ring des Nibelungen* cycle, and to stand in Munich on the bank of the Isar with a grand boulevard and bridge leading to it. But he soon began bitterly to realize that his governess had been right—it was not true that "whatever belongs to my subjects belongs to me." His finance minister denied him the money, and the architect who made the sketches was obliged to sue before he was paid.

PHOTO KEMPTER

Munich, a city of 150,000, already had a large opera house and did not want a new one, especially one for Wagnerian operas. Richard Wagner was the most unpopular man in town. Except for Ludwig, royalists hated Wagner because he had been associated with the revolutionary movements of 1848 and was even thought to have fought at the barricades in Dresden; socialists hated him because he was sheltered under the wing of a would-be absolute ruler; the ordinary citizenry, who cared nothing for politics, was scandalized by Wagner's affair with Cosima von Bülow. Wagner was then fifty-one years old, and his amatory record included an abandoned wife and any number of mistresses, of whom Frau von Bülow was the latest. But the unworldly young King refused to listen to the clamorous gossip and stood by his hero. In fact, he wrote an open letter to the lady's hus-

band, the noted conductor Hans von Bülow, which said, in part: "As I have been in a position to obtain the most intimate knowledge of the character of your honorable wife, it only remains for me to discover the inexplicable reasons for these criminal insults." But people began to call Wagner "Lolus," and the prime minister threatened to resign if Wagner did not leave Munich. Ludwig, the absolute monarch born too late, meekly sent Wagner to live in Switzerland.

Not long after, Ludwig learned beyond a shadow of a doubt that Wagner was indeed the lover of Cosima and the father of the third child in the Von Bülow family. Amazingly, this did not destroy Ludwig's devotion to Wagner, but possibly it impelled him to seek out a relationship with a woman himself. Some months later, he became engaged to his first-cousin-once-removed, Sophie, a pretty, docile Wittelsbach princess whose elder sister, Elizabeth, was the Empress of Austria. Ludwig called her "Elsa," himself "Heinrich." "My dear Elsa!" he wrote to her, "The God of my life, as you know, is Richard Wagner." . . . "My Beloved Elsa! . . . How happy I am to have seen Him again and talked to Him after nine long months." . . . "W. comes to me today at 1 o'clock and we shall have a couple of beautiful hours of cosy talk together; think of Us!" One wonders what Sophie thought of such love letters.

A wedding coach was ordered, painted with scenes of the life of Louis XIV plus a scene of a theater during a performance of a Wagner opera; Sophie was measured for a crown; an elaborate apartment, connected by secret staircase with Ludwig's, was prepared for her in the Munich Residenz. And during the blessedly long time that these things took, Ludwig went off incognito to Paris in the company of his chief groom. Twice the wedding date was postponed; the bride's father was forced to make indignant inquiries; and at last Ludwig wrote Sophie as honest a letter as was possible for him: "Now I have had time to test myself, and think the whole matter over, and I see that my true and faithful brotherly love is now, and always will be, deeply rooted in my soul; but I also see that there is not the love which is necessary for a matrimonial union." In his diary Ludwig noted: "Sophie written off. The gloomy picture fades. . . . Now I live again after this torturing nightmare."

Having closed the doors to a normal life, he was free to hurry down the secret passageways of his own fantastic world. Forthwith he plunged himself into the real passion of his life—building and decorating. His trip to France, where he had seen the Paris Exposition of 1867 as well as Versailles and other royal palaces, seems to have set his imagination flying off in all directions, and the architects' offices of Munich began to burn lights late into the night. Plans were drawn up for a facsimile of Versailles, for a medieval fortress with a Singers' Hall in it like the one in *Tannhäuser*, and for a Moorish-Byzantine palace. The royal apartments in the Munich Residenz were enlarged and decorated lavishly in a late-late-rococo style, and an enormous winter garden, under a vaulted glass roof, was added to the top floor of the Residenz, complete with palm trees, fountains, a pond and a running stream, a blue silk tent, a bamboo hut, a stalactite grotto, and an Oriental kiosk. There were swans (stuffed) and peacocks (real), and a small barque for rowing about; and in the background, a painting of the Himalayas. (A sturdy soprano who had come to the palace ostensibly to discuss a forthcoming opera, but who had hopes of bringing the aloof young man around to more personal subjects, once climbed aboard the barque, upset it, and screamed for help; Ludwig, instead of wading in and seizing her in his arms, rang for footmen and bade his damp visitor good night.)

Schloss Linderhof, begun in 1869, started out to be a little garden chalet like Marly, at Versailles, but when it was completed, ten years later, it was pure Ludwigian. The chief of the architects and decorators was Christian Jank, a Munich stage designer—and certainly Linderhof looks more like a stage set than a place to live. It has only twelve rooms, excepting servants' quarters, and the outstanding impression they all convey is *horror vacui*. The modern eye rebels at the sight of so much clutter. But Ludwig, however much he de-

CONTINUED ON PAGE 125

ANKS—F.P.G.

Ludwig's taste for undisciplined ornament is illustrated by his bed at Neuschwanstein (left) and by the peacock throne in the Moorish kiosk at Linderhof (right). The bed is a Gothic nightmare in oak that took seventeen men some four and a half years to carve, while the peacocks were fabricated of enameled zinc plates studded with bits of colored Bohemian glass.

*"I listen to the music. I listen, listen, listen, listen,
and then it comes: the general idea of what I want. Then I can
begin to move the dancers around."*

*"The male dancer I like to watch, really the only one I like
to watch, is an American—Fred Astaire."*

*"Now we train our bodies to be bone,
to be ascetic. You can dress a skeleton, make it sexy, anything.
But you never know what a fat man is."*

*"Supposing a man and a woman do a fox trot together.
What's abstract about that? We in ballet do just the same thing,
except that we jump better and we look more beautiful."*

BALANCHINE

An interview by

IVAN NABOKOV AND ELIZABETH CARMICHAEL

George Skibine, himself a choreographer, tells a story about George Balanchine: a friend went to him with an idea for a new ballet, a complicated affair involving a husband, his wife, his mistress, and her brother-in-law. Balanchine listened patiently and thoughtfully. Then he said: "In ballet I can tell the audience that a man is in love with a woman, but—alas—there is no choreographic method of showing that the other fellow is her brother-in-law."

The only trouble with this story is that Balanchine, if pressed, probably *could* make his dancers project such a relationship across the footlights. There is no doubt that today he is a choreographer without peer, or that his New York City Ballet is one of the great dance companies of the world. Lacking the resources of the opulent, athletic Bolshoi or of England's silken Royal Ballet, it is more adventurous than either. Its swift, pure, clean-lined style often makes them seem old-fashioned. And it possesses the inestimable advantages of Balanchine's artistic direction and a full repertoire of his ballets, which include some of the authentic masterpieces of the twentieth century. They range in mood and style from the serene classicism of his early *Apollo* (Stravinsky) through subtle evocations of the Romantic era like *Serenade* (Tchaikovsky's Serenade for Strings) to such astringent, witty visions of the future as *Agon* (Stravinsky again).

Balanchine's ballet career started at the age of nine when he was enrolled, more or less by accident (his mother had wanted to put him in a military academy but was told she would have to wait a year), in St. Petersburg's Imperial School of Ballet. He was graduated in 1921 and

ERNST HAAS

Standing before the mirrored wall of his School of American Ballet, George Balanchine observes his company rehearsing Allegro Brillante

entered the famed Maryinsky company as a member of the corps de ballet. In 1924 he left Russia with a small troupe of Maryinsky dancers, who were to perform in Western Europe under the name of the Soviet State Dancers, and never went back. Diaghilev snapped him up for his Ballets Russes and shortly installed him, despite his lack of experience, as ballet master. During these years Balanchine choreographed a number of major works, including two that are still danced by his own company today: *Apollo* and *The Prodigal Son.* On one occasion, as an indication of his versatility, he even subbed for Alicia Markova—just then sixteen—in Stravinsky's *Rossignol*, when she suddenly fell ill. The late Pavel Tchelitchew, who was with the company as a scenic designer and had not been forewarned, turned to Diaghilev when Balanchine appeared on stage and asked in horror: "My God, what's happened to Alicia? She looks like a big, fat rabbit!" Tchelitchew afterwards used to press the unlikely opinion that Balanchine was good enough to get through the performance without being detected by the general audience.

After the death of Diaghilev and the dissolution of his empire into the hands of myriad creditors, Balanchine worked intermittently in London, Copenhagen, Paris, and Monte Carlo. In 1933 he was sought out by Lincoln Kirstein, a wealthy, impulsive young Bostonian mesmerized by the ballet, who wanted to persuade him to come to America and create a native ballet company. Balanchine said he would be delighted to go to a country that produced such wonderful girls as Ginger Rogers. The two men have been associated ever since.

Typical of the dingy world behind the stage, the offices of the New York City Ballet at the City Center are bare, high-ceilinged, ill-lit rooms—rooms as dusty and gloomy as country railroad stations; there is a transitory atmosphere about them, as though they were used to walk quickly through, perhaps to sign a paper or answer a telephone in, and then to leave from gratefully in the evening. When Balanchine arrived for the interview, he sat down quickly in a straight-backed chair and leaned forward, a small man with graceful hands placed in front of him on the table. He has a quick, unqualified smile, a little nod of the head. He dresses in the tight-fitting clothes one associates with the American West, specifically with the elegant gambler at the corner table of the dance hall: black string tie, pearl-buttoned shirt, and frontier trousers. His voice is serious and melodious, with the Russian inflection quite evident (he says that he speaks English "through" Russian). When he's excited his slight body twists on the chair in a mime of pleasure or outrage.

46

INTERVIEWER: How do you go about developing a ballet?

BALANCHINE: I know the music; I choose it; I listen to it. I listen, listen, listen, listen, and then it comes: the general idea of what I want, perhaps how the ballet begins and ends—all of this suggested by the music—how many dancers, and the costumes, and so forth. But it is not until the dancers are on the stage and I am with them that I can begin. Then I can move them around. It's like building a sculpture, you see. You have the clay there, and you work on it, molding it, changing it, shaping it, until you have what you want.

INTERVIEWER: But don't you start with some theme or idea, perhaps, that you've long been eager to realize?

BALANCHINE: No, no. You see, it's not like necessity; I'm not so excited or hungry to tell people something. What I must do is supply my restaurant with a *plat du jour.* I have to "feed" people because we charge them money. They come and pay $2.95 or $3.95, whatever it is, and we have to give them something to look at. That's my job. So I never know ahead of time what I'm going to do. I have to calculate. If I've already given them something American, something modern, or something Russian, like Tchaikovsky or Rimsky-Korsakov or Stravinsky, then I may decide that I must have something French, either old or modern. Or maybe it should be an English or a Japanese ballet. I do something like that. You have to calculate your menu. Like planning a meal, you have to have this and this and that.

INTERVIEWER: But isn't a specific idea or story the starting point for most choreographers?

BALANCHINE: Perhaps. In France, for instance, people are very intellectual, and ballets there are always based on a literary idea. Their choreography is poor because they emphasize the secondary aspects of ballet. Somebody writes a libretto, usually a second-rate writer, and a ballet is built around it. You recall those lengthy program notes explaining the performance to be given; the comments are so many and so involved that one never really understands them. Yet in France the libretto, secondary in my opinion, is considered as important as the choreography. Fifteen per cent of the gross taken in always goes to the Société des Auteurs et Compositeurs Dramatiques. There a ballet is first of all the subject, *le sujet.* The French want to know what a

Another in the HORIZON interview series
THE ARTIST SPEAKS FOR HIMSELF
under the editorship of George Plimpton

ballet represents, what it means. People never seem to understand unless they can put their finger into things. Like touching dough—when people see bread rising, they smell something and they say, "Oh, is it going up?" And they poke their finger in it. "Ah," they say, "now I see." But of course the dough then goes down. They spoil everything by insisting on touching. That's why, when you go to museums, you see signs saying PLEASE DON'T TOUCH. People have to be told "don't touch" because they won't believe their eyes. And with music, too—they want to know what a particular sound means. "Ah, it's a storm," they say, and think they understand. It's the same with ballet—they want to know why a ballerina is doing a particular *pas seul* or why a man and a woman are doing some dance together. They're not satisfied without an explanation—unless they can say that a ballet is abstract. To them the word "abstract" means that a ballet has no story. But a realistic part of life could very well not have a story. You don't have to explain a chair. You might say that Washington sat there, but you don't *have* to say anything at all. And a chair isn't abstract because you don't have to talk about it—it is just *there.*

INTERVIEWER: From the point of view of such a public, the perfect abstract ballet would be one in which all the parts could be danced interchangeably by men or women?

BALANCHINE: They wouldn't know what to think. And they would settle their doubts by saying, "You see, this is an abstract ballet." But I say that such a ballet is not abstract. It is concrete. Concrete because you see people, a man and a woman. They are there, they are present. Why must that signify something more? Supposing a man and a woman go to a restaurant. After they have had a nice dinner, they do a fox trot together. What's abstract about that? You don't write a story about it. They dance, perhaps, for the pleasure of dancing. They hear music and they enjoy tapping the floor and being with the time. We in ballet do just the same thing, except that perhaps we do it a little faster and a little better. We jump better and we look more beautiful.

INTERVIEWER: Then you think that the story or idea is secondary, that music is the most important aspect of the ballet?

BALANCHINE: Yes, because music is more perfect time than we can make. Man's body is very slow. We divide time slowly. Our body can make only large divisions because we have only two legs and two arms—four parts, and the head makes five. Actually, we can hardly move. Music could be divided faster than it is. The way music is made now it has sixty-four divisions, you know —whole, half, quarter, eighth, sixteenth, thirty-second, and sixty-fourth notes—as fast as fingers can play, many more movements than a dancer's body can produce. But we don't need to make so many movements. It is enough that we should be able to occupy a portion of time at one particular moment. We try, in the most interesting way, to swim in time. Music is time. It's not the melody that's important but the division of time.

INTERVIEWER: Do you think you could ever do a ballet that had its own time—in other words, that had no music?

BALANCHINE: No, I couldn't make a ballet without music. I am not a creator of time myself. I like to be subordinated to it. Only a musician is a creator of time. Stravinsky is a creator of wonderful time—a little man who invents wonderful time. In my life I have known only a few who could make those very interesting moments of time that you felt like swimming in. You know, like a little swimming pool that you are so happy to be inside of. I couldn't do that, it's not my job. Well, you can't do two things. Mr. Stravinsky provides me with wonderful time, and I like to swim in it. I couldn't make time for him, and if I could, he wouldn't know how to move in it.

INTERVIEWER: Who thought of making *Apollo*? Was it Stravinsky's idea or was it yours?

BALANCHINE: It was Stravinsky's idea. He wrote it in America for Mrs. Elizabeth Sprague Coolidge. She commissioned it, and he wrote this classical, Handel type of music, *Apollon Musagète* [*Apollo, Leader of the Muses*, now called simply *Apollo*]. Instead of nine muses he used just three, because nine are very boring—every muse is the same. So he took the most prominent ones—the muses of poetry, drama, and dance—just to have some pretext, and on those he made variations.

INTERVIEWER: In the ballets you've done with Stravinsky—*Apollo, Orpheus,* and *Agon,* for instance—did you work with him before he composed the music or while he was writing it?

BALANCHINE: Only afterwards, because the music is always first. I cannot move, I don't even want to move, unless I hear the music first. I couldn't move without a reason, and the reason is music. Ballet likes to move in time, inside of this calculated time—to swim in it, you see. And if you don't have it, there is no reason to do anything. That's how it is for me. I was trained that way; my muscles only move when time comes in. When it is not there, I am dead. Some people think we improvise. You may improvise in imagination, perhaps, but then you have to pin down and to clarify. It's like writing a book. The first flow of words has to be reworked. You have to eliminate many things until you get exactly what you want. It should be like building a little

house that will stand over your head for a long time and won't collapse. That's what we do. We just can't dance for pleasure like a person who screams "I'm happy, I'm happy!" That's all right for the person who's happy. But for the other guy it's nothing. Of course there are modern dancers who express themselves differently from us. First they have a thought, they feel something. They put gesture into that. Let's suppose a person feels very happy. He feels very happy because his mother has passed away, perhaps, or because he can say, "I am free today" or "My stomach is working—last night it didn't, today it does." There is always a reason for physical happiness. People feel happy and start dancing. Still, they feel it with the body, and that is where they put their gesture—trying to imitate their feelings. That's how they work, just opposite to me; first they put on the ballet, they move around, and then the other fellow writes the music.

INTERVIEWER: In connection with dancing of this sort, did you ever see Isadora Duncan?

BALANCHINE: Yes, I saw her in Russia in 1920 or '21. I thought she was awful. I don't understand it when people say she was a great dancer. To me it was absolutely unbelievable—a drunken, fat woman who for hours was rolling around like a pig. It was the most awful thing. It is unbelievable how people can be hypnotized so nobody dares to say what he thinks. I don't believe that she ever danced well. She was probably a nice juicy girl when she was young. When I saw her in 1920, I don't know exactly how old she was—probably forty. There was no reason to be so bad at forty. I can't believe she was excellent when she was thirty. Those ten years couldn't have made such a difference.

INTERVIEWER: With regard to your own work, are there any composers or types of music that you find unchoreographable?

BALANCHINE: I wouldn't call them unchoreographable, but I would say that it is better not to use some of them. For instance, I wouldn't use Beethoven's overtures because they are made for listening. I wouldn't know what to do with them.

INTERVIEWER: Could you work with chamber music—something like, say, the Schubert Quintet in C?

BALANCHINE: It's too long. It could be used, but that kind of music is too long; it repeats itself all the time. It is made for people to enjoy playing more than for people to listen to. It's like games. Games are much more interesting to people who actually participate. Take Monopoly: you watch four people play like mad for hours, and while they are at it they don't even know you exist. They don't give a damn what happens to you. "Look at me—I'm around

here, I'm present, too!" But no, they are so involved. Of course you can watch them, see how they enjoy it, but they are having a better time. So I would say that quintets and quartets are better for people who actually play them than for those who sit and listen.

INTERVIEWER: What about part of the Quintet?

BALANCHINE: *Part* of a quintet—you mean the Schubert double cello quintet? It's a beautiful thing; everybody remembers the slow movement, but the rest of it is so long. What are you going to do with the beginning and the end? But you could use it if necessary. I would say that you could use anything Mozart ever wrote, from beginning to end—every song, every overture, every opera, every symphony—you can dance to all of it. As for Brahms, you can't dance to very much of his music; it's written mostly to be listened to or to be performed. His symphonies, for instance—Massine did a ballet to the Fourth Symphony, but I think it was a mess. It's impossible to use that music in two different ways—to be both played and danced to—impossible. Besides, it's so sticky. You have to be *free* to play it, and you are not free if you have to accompany a dance at the same time. No, Brahms won't do as an accompaniment for dancing, except for the waltzes. The Liebeslieder Waltzes are nice to dance to—they're really waltzy. Stravinsky—anything he writes can be danced to. He's like Mozart to me. Stravinsky and Mozart have the same kind of timing. Their time has a quality that one can move in. The same is true of Verdi. You can dance to everything that he wrote—every opera, every overture, every ensemble. Gounod can be danced, and Tchaikovsky and Delibes and Bizet. I think Bach can also be used.* Bach is really written for activity. His music is written for a purpose, to accompany something, either words or feelings—for instance, the church service. So I would say that one can use any kind of music if necessary, but *I* wouldn't.

INTERVIEWER: Would you do a ballet to something like Mahler's Fifth Symphony?

BALANCHINE: If you paid me, yes. If you said I'll give you a million dollars, I'd say Fine, I'll do something, I'll struggle. But I wouldn't do it for nothing. Not that I don't like him—Mahler is a very good composer. But I wouldn't use him for a ballet. The same is true for Bruckner.

INTERVIEWER: What about Bartók?

BALANCHINE: You could use certain things. His time is not very interesting to move in. I would say that Bartók's time is primitive; rhythmically it's very banal.

*One of Balanchine's best ballets, *Concerto Barocco*, is set to Bach's Concerto in D minor for two violins.

Schönberg is more interesting, and Hindemith, too.

INTERVIEWER: But is Hindemith very interesting rhythmically?

BALANCHINE: Rhythmically no, but there is a little bit more of a circusy thing about him. I mean that he writes certain things with a special end in view; he could write music for the circus. He can do anything, you know. It's like *musique d'ameublement,* as Satie used to say, like movie music—you can do things with it.

INTERVIEWER: Once you've supplied your audience with a ballet, are you satisfied with it, or do you continue to tinker with it after it's opened?

BALANCHINE: It takes time to adapt ourselves to it, like wearing a new suit. There are people involved, you see, and music and bodies and proportions; and though we work as fast as possible, there isn't enough time before we open—so afterward we must continue to adapt ourselves.

INTERVIEWER: Do you make major changes?

BALANCHINE: No, I don't want to make changes as much as to polish and perfect what we already have. You cannot squeeze out more orange juice than there is—even though people expect you to. When I finish a ballet, sometimes I feel more achievement, sometimes less. But I cannot start by saying, "I will produce a revelation no matter what." It doesn't happen.

INTERVIEWER: Does that mean that each completed ballet entails a certain disappointment on your part because you did not produce a "revelation?"

BALANCHINE: Not for me. I suppose it would for many people. The trouble is that everyone wants to do the major work. No one starts modestly. What I think is that you have to use everything life gives you—like opening an icebox and reaching inside—and you use it well and modestly and hope that you're a little better at it than you were yesterday. Since you are being judged by an audience, you must supply them, not with a fantastic dinner every day, but sometimes with a glass of milk. We're not showing off, you see—ballet must be entertaining so that an audience can appreciate it.

INTERVIEWER: Is it difficult to evaluate a ballet performance?

BALANCHINE: Well, so often the critical evaluation is misplaced. The balletomanes, for example, are usually amateurs with predigested opinions about the ballet and its stars. Their forefathers were those who bought tickets in the *premier rang* in the old days, the Officers of the Guard—the plumed hats, the swords, the great bouquets of flowers sent backstage—admirers not of the dance but of the dancer. There is no *premier rang* today. The balletomanes are the nearest thing to it, but they are not so good. The true audience are the connoisseurs, the students, the intelligentsia who see what you offer in its proper perspective. They are either pleased or disappointed by the offering, but at least they are seeing the presentation in its whole, as it is supposed to be seen. I never think of the commercial value of anything I do—I mean the audience does not dictate what I do—but still I think of this audience and how I can entertain it: even *Agon*, though new, obviously, and unfamiliar, is nevertheless gay, it's amusing, and it is dancing.

INTERVIEWER: Does it bother you that ballet is so ephemeral an art—that even after you've perfected a dance it remains only in memory once it is dropped from the repertoire?

BALANCHINE: Actually, there is a way to get choreography down for posterity—an invention called the Laban System of Dance Notation. But, in fact, I can see no need for preservation. A ballet is a movement in time and space, a living moment. Like a hothouse flower, it blooms, then dies. A ballet is life. It is not architecture or a column that stands forever or a painting, but something which belongs to the people who execute it, to their bodies. A music score is constant; it stays as it is written, and the only change is in performance. Mozart would delight to hear his music played today. But the ballet is not music, it is movement; and movement by its nature exists only in time. That is as it should be. Who wishes to see last year's butterflies? Bodies change, people are taller. In the Maryinsky Theatre, when I started, the girls stood in rows sixteen deep, and they were short and plump, with busts and corsets, and they wore their hair up. They were the ones who were the delight of the *premier rang*. They were like those fat nudes on the balustrades of the Paris Opéra and painted on its ceilings—the place looks like a glorified whore house, you know, or at the very least a Turkish bath. But times have changed. Now we train our bodies to be bone, to be ascetic. Bone is personality, fat is pancake. You can dress a skeleton, make it sexy, anything. You can say, Ah, that person is so-and-so or such-and-such, but you never know what a fat man is.

INTERVIEWER: Other than that, what do you look for in a dancer? If, like Pygmalion, you could mold a dancer, what proportions and skills would you give her?

BALANCHINE: If I could do such a thing, the chances are that my dancer couldn't move. The ideal dancer would be a monster. I believe a magazine tried to do that once—a composite beauty made up of Garbo's eyes, someone's nose, someone else's neck—and it was a nobody. You see, in the ballet you never can tell. A long foot can compensate for the shortness of a leg. Sometimes you see a body and you say it's not beautiful. But then she moves, and the mechanics of her moving produce an impression of beauty. On the other hand, Miss America starts to move and it is ugliness. So what you look for in a dancer is what she can give you. There is nothing more you can do. You cannot supply that sort of talent—which is sublime—but only the technique for using it.

INTERVIEWER: There is no characteristic common to them all?

BALANCHINE: There is a certain flexibility—and swiftness. I can recognize them maybe a couple of years in advance. Sometimes people tell me, No, no, she's no good; and I say, Perhaps, perhaps. I enjoy the student, you know, the one who always wants to learn different things. I want a dancer to be perfect, but if she is wrong, I don't mind. It is all right to be consciously wrong, but not right to be unconsciously wrong. That is what you must teach—to *know* what is right.

INTERVIEWER: Is nationality characterized in the dancer?

BALANCHINE: Well, when I first started teaching in this country, the men dancers, who don't start early enough here, found the necessary gestures of the ballet difficult to make. They told me I embarrassed them, made them feel silly—this gesture, that gesture, the hand held so, the arm that way. I told them that baseball embarrassed *me*—the pitcher leaning back and raising his leg up like that—why couldn't he throw the ball without those terrible gestures? So we are even, no? But I will tell you something that maybe will make you laugh. It should not. I am serious. The male dancer I like to watch, really the only one I like to watch, is an American—Fred Astaire. He is the most interesting, the most inventive, the most elegant dancer of our times. I don't mean classical, of course, but *dancing*; he's so good at it that he ought to have a statue. I mean that absolutely. The beauty of his body—I've not seen him undressed, but he must be very, very thin, all bones—the way he moves, his elegance, his dancing . . . he is saying, Look, ma, I'm dancing! He is terribly rare. He is like Bach, who in his time had a great concentration of ability, essence, knowledge, a spread of music. Astaire has that same concentration of genius; there is so much of the dance in him that it has been distilled. You see a little bit of Astaire in everybody's dancing—a pause here, a move there. It was all Astaire's originally.

INTERVIEWER: Have you ever worked with Astaire?

BALANCHINE: No. I only met him two or three times, out in Hollywood when I was working there.

INTERVIEWER: Didn't you have a project out there with George Gershwin to make a film of *An American in Paris?*

BALANCHINE: That's how we started, but then Gershwin died.

INTERVIEWER: Did you ever get any of it made?

BALANCHINE: No. I wish we had because it would have been the first example of a ballet made especially for the screen. It would have been a wonderful thing, but Goldwyn wouldn't allow us to start because he was afraid it might not turn out right. He wanted to see the whole thing *right then,* in one place, without going around on the set and picking up the pieces—which is what movie-making really is. That's why we made the water-nymph ballet for *The Goldwyn Follies* instead of *An American in Paris.* Goldwyn said he wanted to see right in front of his eyes what was going to happen, so we made something he could put his chair in front of: a pool with columns, and Brigitta * in a beautiful gold thing that came out of the water, and in the middle a big horse which I made like a De Chirico horse. Goldwyn's one criticism was, "I don't like this horse; it's not human." Jascha Heifetz was on the set preparing some movie—*One Hundred Men and a Girl,* I think it was—with Stokowski. He doesn't know it, but he saved my horse, because Goldwyn asked him, "Jascha, look at that horse. What do you think?" And Jascha said, "I love it; I think it's wonderful." So Goldwyn said, "Come on, shoot!" If Jascha hadn't been there, the horse wouldn't have stayed either; and if we hadn't had the horse—it was the main thing—we really wouldn't have had anything.

INTERVIEWER: Goldwyn must have been difficult to work with.

BALANCHINE: He's a very nice man, actually, and sincere, and he makes acute remarks. He's a very bright man. But he didn't tell me anything much because at that time I didn't speak English well—not that I speak it well now, but at least now I could make him understand me. Before, probably, he couldn't understand a word I was saying. I remember once when George Gershwin and his brother Ira, and Goldwyn and I, were sitting around conversing. George spoke to me in a very strange way, so strange that even Ira said, "George, what kind of language are you using? Even Balanchine doesn't understand what you

*Brigitta Hartwig, better known as Vera Zorina—one of the five beautiful ballerinas who have been Balanchine's wives. The others are Tamara Geva, whom he married before he left Russia and who later starred in a number of Broadway musicals; Alexandra Danilova, the great prima ballerina of the Ballet Russe de Monte Carlo; Maria Tallchief, one of the best dancers in the world today; and his present wife, Tanaquil LeClercq, a dazzling young ballerina who was tragically stricken with polio in 1956.

are saying." It was almost like Chinese. He would say, "If–me–you–together," like pidgin English, or maybe Tarzan. Of course I could understand English better than George thought I could. Goldwyn was sitting there trying to explain that he thought I was too advanced, that I couldn't understand this movie business, that he was afraid to spend $100,000 on a ballet when I didn't know anything yet about movie-making. But, frankly, I must say that I learned very quickly—it's not such a puzzle. And when we made a couple of test shots and put them together, Goldwyn was amazed. "Wonderful," he said, "really amazing and beautiful"; then he said, "All right, let's do it." He didn't interfere any more. Anybody can learn. You go to the cutting room, you learn how to assemble things, and so on.

INTERVIEWER: How did you get into musical comedy? Was *On Your Toes* your first musical?

BALANCHINE: No. *Ziegfeld Follies.* After Ziegfeld died, the Shuberts took over. Lots of the people in it were very important, but I didn't know anybody except Josephine Baker. I knew her from Europe. I was still European, you see; I had just come to America from Diaghilev, and I had some kind of reputation. I know who wanted me —it was John Murray Anderson, the Englishman who directed the whole thing. I did several ballets for Josephine Baker; she was very beautiful at that time. She had a wonderful body and she was a lovely singer. I think she was the best in the show, but they didn't like her because she was American. If she had been French, they would have gone wild; but an American Negro from Harlem—people said, Who the hell is she, who does she think she is? And she really was wonderful: a wonderful woman, a wonderful singer, a beautiful voice, really talented, but she couldn't do anything here because she was American.

INTERVIEWER: You saw the two big Soviet companies when they were here—the Moiseyev and the Bolshoi—and you also met Moiseyev. What did you think?

BALANCHINE: I had a little lunch with Moiseyev. Sol Hurok arranged it, but lots of people were present. There was a big table; I was far away from Moiseyev. I talked to his wife, who sat next to me. I commented on the wonderful wine Hurok served—he's very generous—some fantastic thing like Mouton-Rothschild '47, you know, the best. And I told Mrs. Moiseyev how really the best wine in the world is the French wine, how Bordeaux is the king of wines. And she said No, not at all, Russian wine is the best. I asked her *which* Russian wine, and she said Caucasian wine. I said I knew it very well because my father came

TEXT CONTINUED ON PAGE 56

ON THE NEXT SIX PAGES

THE NEW YORK CITY BALLET

PHOTOGRAPHS BY ERNST HAAS

Two ballets that show Balanchine's range are Agon *and* The Figure in the Carpet. *They could hardly be more unlike.* Agon *(Plate I) is set to one of Stravinsky's most advanced scores and is danced in the stark black leotards that have become almost the "uniform" of the New York City Ballet. Crisp, angular, and almost reckless in its movement, it has the dry, exhilarating sparkle of the very best champagne* brut. *There is sparkle, too, in* The Figure in the Carpet, *but since it is danced to Handel's* Water Music *it is of quite a different kind. Its first part, called "The Sands of the Desert" (Plate II), is flowing and romantic in mood. Its second half is a brilliant spectacle such as might have been put on at the court of Louis XIV. And at the end, when the entire cast is massed on stage for a low, sweeping bow (Plate III), their lavish—even extravagant—costumes make a pattern as colorful as the Persian carpet that Balanchine says was the inspiration for the whole thing.*

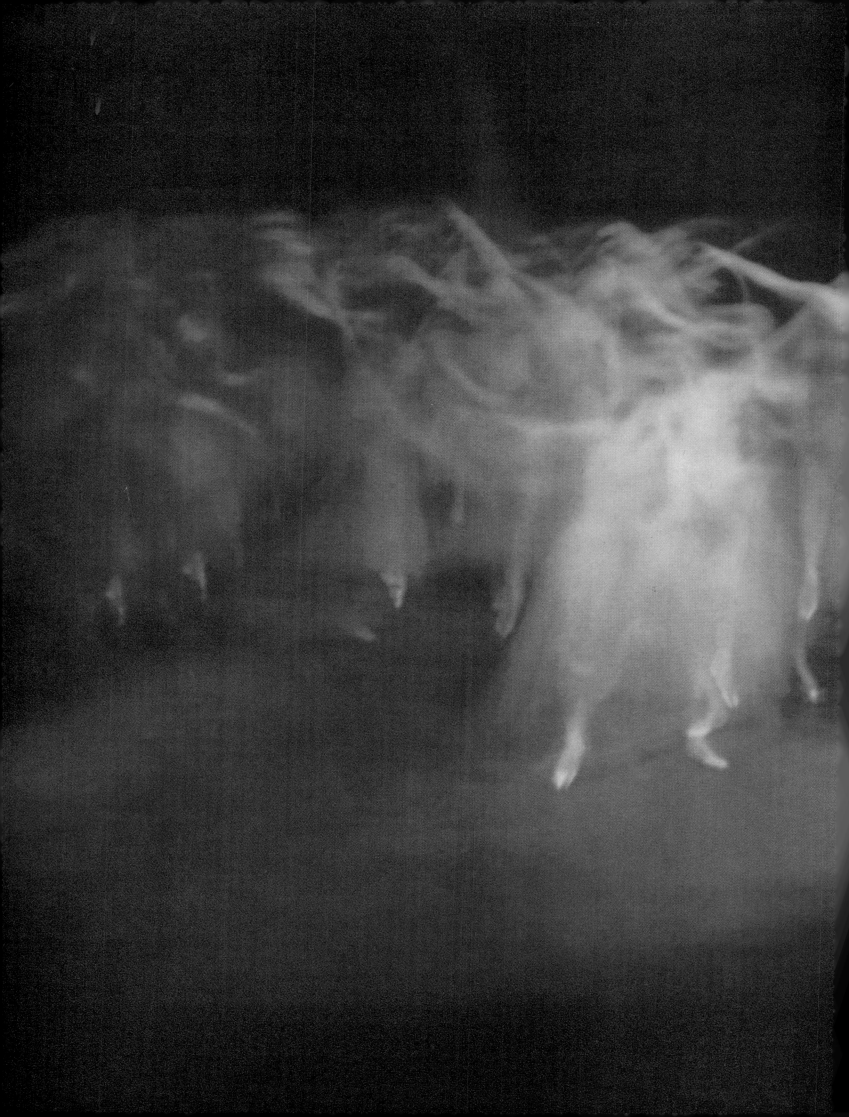

TEXT CONTINUED FROM PAGE 49

from there. Russian wine is not so bad, you know. It's like California wine, *not so bad.* But she said, "Oh, you have no idea what's going on now. The Soviet people have improved. And now Caucasian wine is the greatest wine." So I really didn't have a chance to talk to anybody. I talked a bit to the Bolshoi's head choreographer, Leonid Lavrovsky. He was my friend and we lived together before the Revolution. We even slept next to each other in a sort of dormitory. Unfortunately, he couldn't say much. If we had started a serious discussion on what art is, he would probably have been sent away to Siberia. We only reminisced a little bit about the past, how we used to live, and so on.

INTERVIEWER: Do you see any young choreographers who have the same conception of ballet as you do?

BALANCHINE: I don't know—people don't work any more. They don't try to make anything; they want to be produced at once. They won't make a move until they know something will happen. Everybody always says "my creation," but I say that nobody can create except God. Creation is by God. *We* just assemble things that already exist. But you really have to do a lot of things before you become somebody. Writers have to write something before they become anybody. It's easy for editors because they just throw away lots of paper.* For choreographers it's difficult because they have to use people. And yet it could be done. I wish we could find someone, but nobody I know of is really doing anything, or very little. They try; there are some professional types of people who assemble things, but they make nothing very unusual because they don't work, they don't sacrifice their time. They want to sell immediately. As they say in Russian, "As soon as they spit, manna should fall from Heaven."

INTERVIEWER: Would you ever do another project like your staging of Gluck's *Orpheus and Eurydice* at the Metropolitan in 1936, when you put the singers in the orchestra pit and had only dancers on the stage?

BALANCHINE: No, I wouldn't do it again. The music is very beautiful, but it already exists—you don't have to force it. Besides, we did it once. So much energy was put into it, and it was very beautiful, but people didn't understand—the public did, but the administration and the critics didn't. Part of my life went into it and I just couldn't do it again. I enjoy playing the score now, alone. But I wouldn't stage an opera that way a second time. I like the opera of Verdi; I like the singing, but really I don't care how it's staged. The singers may look fat and old, they may

*That's what he thinks.—ED.

wear beards and be funnily dressed—it doesn't hurt the music. Verdi is a great man, and the voice and the orchestra are quite enough as it is. He wrote for singers who were short and squat. They played an imaginary Aïda or Nebuchadnezzar looking like fat Italian spaghetti cooks. But who cares? It doesn't matter at all. Even for *opera seria,* costume doesn't make much difference.

INTERVIEWER: But you emphasized costumes when you made *The Figure in the Carpet* last spring.

BALANCHINE: Yes, we used costumes. But it's a ballet—that's the difference. Even in Soviet Russia when a girl dances on points she is covered with feathers and diamonds. I don't know how they justify it. Is it the memory of a beautiful sparkling past, or is it something else? Lunacharsky persuaded Lenin that he had to keep this art—that it would lure people into theaters where you could convince them. So before performances they had propagandists telling about dialectical materialism; then they showed a little bit of dance. Still, the audience wore white shirts, they cleaned themselves up to come.

INTERVIEWER: If resources were unlimited and there were a government-subsidized theater, what would be the ideal setup from your point of view?

BALANCHINE: If resources were unlimited—which is impossible—I think the most important things would be, first, to have lots of good seats so that people can see properly, a good space for the orchestra, and a sufficient number of musicians who can play. Not a small orchestra, because that limits the choice of music; one can't play certain pieces. I would like to have a small symphony. A seventy-man orchestra would be enough. Then I would like to have good light and enough space behind the scenes so that we could hide in the wings when we run off stage. Then we should have a sufficient number of dancers —not just twenty boys and twenty girls as we have now so that if one person in a group falls sick, you have to make do with nineteen. I would like twenty-five in a group, so that five could rest during a particular ballet and take over afterward if something happened. And better pay for the dancers. Dancers are very, very poorly paid—worse than anyone. First of all, they are not paid the whole year round; they may work only thirty weeks a year. If you consider that they get only $90 before taxes, so that with taxes taken off they get only $70 a week for thirty weeks, that makes only $2,000 a year! Some elevator men complain they make only $4,000 a year. But we are good-natured people and we like our work. I would say that if we could be paid a little more, just a little more, about

double what we are getting now, if a dancer could be paid $4,000 a year, he would be very happy. And if we could get musicians, a little more space, and production funds so that we wouldn't have to hesitate to order so many pairs of shoes and clean tights, that would be fine. I wouldn't even dream of anything else. I wouldn't want to spend hundreds of thousands on a production—I wouldn't know how. I don't want people to be overdressed, nor do I want a marble staircase or gold knobs. Reinhardt, I remember, had real gold doorknobs in his productions. Ten thousand dollars went just for knobs. In the Maryinsky Theatre in the old days, every week or so in a Moussorgsky opera they burned down a two-story house that you could have lived in. But we don't want that. We're not very expensive, really.

INTERVIEWER: Do you believe in a state-subsidized ballet?

BALANCHINE: I believe in it absolutely, but not only for the ballet, for the theater also. Every art should be subsidized. In America the government cannot spend money on the arts without the consent of the people. But the people should *want* to spend money on the arts, and they should be helped spiritually and intellectually by the government. The beauty of this country, you see, is that it is a money country! Everything can be bought—except soul. We can buy all the soap we want, it's very cheap. But after we're very clean, after we've eaten lots of butter and milk and we feel a bit sleepy, we don't know what to do with ourselves. You hear people say, "I want to kill my time; I don't know what to do with it." I say, "Give it to me, I don't have enough." Unfortunately, you can't exchange things like that. That's where the soul comes in. But nobody advertises soul. Nobody even mentions it, and that's what we lack. We lack the awareness, not the feeling. For there *are* people, lots of nice people, who *pack* the City Center, because even if they're poor, it's not very expensive for them and they can spend three hours looking at something nice—we have a beautiful orchestra and wonderful dancers. And I feel sure that eventually such people will get together.

You see, the power of admiring things, which exists, is lost because everybody is doing it on his own and for nothing. Every once in awhile people agree. We meet and we say, "Do you see that little flower? How beautiful it is." "Yes, I see." Well, let us be people who look at flowers together. Let us have a million people saying that a rose is a beautiful shade of pink. There must be organization and agreement between all of us who love beautiful things. And when fifty million people will say loudly, "I love this beautiful thing," the power will be there.

Professor Toynbee tells how he tried and failed
to fit the universal churches into his pattern of
the rise and fall of civilizations

THE HISTORIAN'S STRUGGLE WITH RELIGION

In the first six volumes of *A Study of History,* published before World War II, Arnold Toynbee proposed a cyclical pattern to explain the rise and fall of the twenty-odd civilizations which, by his count, have existed since man emerged from primitive culture. According to this pattern, when a civilization begins to disintegrate it gives birth to a universal state, and this in turn provides the matrix for the rise of a universal religion. Toynbee saw the universal religion as the chrysalis out of which, in time, would come a successor civilization. Thus, in European history, Hellenic civilization produced the Roman Empire which became the matrix for the Christian religion; the Christian church then served as the chrysalis out of which, a thousand years later, came Modern Western Civilization.

When Toynbee published four additional volumes in 1954, his readers were surprised to discover that he had drastically altered his view of universal churches. He now viewed the church not simply as a part of a civilization nor even as a chrysalis to bridge civilizations, but as a separate entity with its own higher ends. The purpose of a civilization, he now seemed to be saying, was to bring forth, in its own disintegration, a universal church.

Toynbee's views, on this and other subjects, have drawn heavy fire from other scholars. In the light of these criticisms and his own further thoughts, he is now at work on an extra volume of *A Study of History,* entitled *Reconsiderations,* to be published next spring. In the following article, which will be part of this volume, he discusses the development of his thought on the subject of religion in history and the personal position to which it has led him.

By ARNOLD J. TOYNBEE

When he undertakes the study of human affairs the historian commits himself, by the act, to becoming a theologian, too. In consternation he may try to beat a retreat from this perilously exposed position into the dead ground of "comparative religion," in the hope that he can escape from theology under the scientific camouflage of anthropological research. But theology is an incubus that a humanist can never shake off. He may seek refuge from theism in atheism or from animism in materialism. But after each desperate twist and turn, he will find himself committed to some theological position or other. Theology is inescapable, and it is dynamite. It will betray its identity through the camouflage by exploding in the end.

In more than one society, at some stage in its history, there have been sceptics who have broken with the world-wide traditional belief that religion—at any rate, one's own religion—is true and valuable. But these earlier accesses of scepticism did not spread beyond rather narrow circles within the societies in which they made their appearance, and they were also relatively short-lived by comparison with the duration of those societies themselves. In retrospect, however, these previous cases take on significance as premonitory symptoms of a sceptical movement which started in the modern Western World in the seventeenth century of the Christian Era and which, since then, has not only gone from strength to strength on its native ground but has spread over the rest of the World in the train of Western Civilization's recent world-wide expansion. This modern Western sceptical movement originated in a moral reaction against the *odium theologicum* that had provided fuel for the so-called "Wars of Religion." Men of good will deliberately took their treasure out of religious controversy and put it into scientific research, which seemed to promise to be a more innocent and also a more fruitful activity. Since then, the findings of scientific research have seemed to undermine the intellectual foundations of traditional religion; and this second blow, following on the moral discredit that the Western Wars of Religion had brought upon religion itself, has now carried religious belief to a perhaps unprecedentedly low ebb.

For the historian the problem is acute because the sceptical-minded and the religious-minded student of human affairs are both living in the same world and addressing themselves to the same public, while at the same time the outlook of each of them seems, from the other's standpoint, to make human affairs unintelligible. For the religious-minded inquirer religion is the highest form of human activity. It offers Man the greatest opportunity of gaining insight into Reality, and of entering into contact with it, that is open to him in this life. Conversely, for the sceptical-minded inquirer a rational understanding of Reality is made impossible by the believer's contention that the essence of Reality is a spiritual presence which from the rationalist's point of view is imaginary.

The historian's journey
from faith to reason,
and beyond . . .
the search for a common ground
between believers
and rationalists

Can we find any common ground between two points of view when the assumptions in which these are respectively grounded are concerned with the very essence of Reality and at the same time appear, to human minds within the present limits of their powers of understanding, to be in diametrical opposition to each other? Perhaps a bare foothold of common ground can be obtained if we can win a concession from either side.

Believers might be asked to meet rationalists part way by agreeing to leave the transhuman presence or presences, in whose existence and potency they believe, out of account when they are engaged in the common enterprise of trying to explain the course of human events and to analyze the structure of human society and the configurations of human culture. It is true that in the pre-rationalist age historians as well as poets treated the reported occurrences of allegedly "supernatural" phenomena on a par with reports of human actions. Accounts of omens, miracles, and the epiphanies and physical intervention of gods were interwoven with accounts of human debates, decisions, agreements, conflicts, achievements, and failures, as if these two elements in the pre-rationalist historians' picture of the course of events were, in principle, equally credible. The reality of the "supernatural" element was simply taken for granted. But, when once the rationalists have challenged this assumption, the onus of proving it surely lies on the shoulders of the believers. They need not be asked to repudiate their traditional assumption; they need merely be asked to refrain—unless and until they can prove it—from continuing to make it when they are engaged in recording, examining, and analyzing human affairs.

As a matter of fact, this concession has been made, in practice, by historians who have not renounced their belief in the existence and potency of transhuman spiritual presences. The reports of miraculous occurrences in terms of polytheistic religious beliefs were repudiated by Jewish, Christian, and Muslim historians long before the modern Western rationalist movement started. Since then, modern historians who have continued to be believing monotheists have tacitly taken to treating the miraculous element in their own religions' picture of human affairs as they have long since treated it overtly in the polytheistic presentation of it. Without repudiating their own belief in the existence and potency of a spiritual presence higher than Man, they have given up their former practice of introducing into their accounts and explanations of human affairs anything of a "supernatural" order.

The reciprocal concession to believers that rationalists might be asked to make is to recognize that rational explanation is imperfect and incomplete, not merely in practice, but intrinsically. Thinking is an attempt to apprehend Reality by catching it in a conceptual net, and a net is able to serve its purpose in virtue of having a texture which leaves gaps between the meshes. It is this open texture which gives a net its fling. If the net were made, not of an open network, but of a tightly woven cloth, the material would be too heavy to allow a net made of it to be effectively extensive. But the price of having a texture which makes it possible to catch something in the net's meshes is the inevitability that something else will slip out of the net through the gaps.

There are, in short, more things in Heaven and Earth than are dreamed of in the rationalist's philosophy, and he cannot be sure that the draught which is let through by the chinks in his system may not be the importunate wind which bloweth where it listeth and which, though it may be invisible to the rationalist's eyes, makes in the believer's ear a sound that, for him, fills the World. The believer may fairly ask the rationalist to meet him to the extent, not of renouncing his rational objective, but of making the negative concession of recognizing that human history, in Christopher Dawson's words, "is impatient of . . . neat systems of laws and causal sequences" for which the rationalist "is always looking," and that the "mysterious and unpredictable aspect of history" is a genuine and irremovable "stumbling-block" for him.

On the other hand, I think that an inquirer who holds, as I myself hold, that rationalism is not enough ought nonetheless to follow the rationalists' good example of recognizing that the human reason's mental net is binding insofar as it is truly effective in apprehending Reality. If I stand convicted (and I have no doubt that I do) of having sometimes lapsed from reasoning into mythologizing when reasoning would have been capable of doing the job, I admit that I have been at fault. At the same time, I am alive to the limitations of human reasoning power, and I am convinced that there are questions which reasoning cannot answer but which human beings are nevertheless bound to ask, because one would be less than human if one did not ask them and did not go on to try to answer them, even though one's answers to such "transrational" questions will be, by definition, unverifiable.

The point of view here described is, of course, a personal one, but I have ventured to describe it, nevertheless, because I think that it brings out the point on which the current controversy between rationalists and "transrationalists" turns. I am, myself, an ex-believer who first became a convert to rationalism with no reservations and has since become a convert to a "transrationalist" standpoint. I am now more alive than I once was to the limitations of human reasoning powers. I believe that answers to the questions that matter most to us can be found only beyond the reason's limits, if they can be found at all. So I am no longer entitled to call myself a rationalist if the label commits one to holding that human reasoning powers are capable of answering all questions that one needs to ask or of proving, for instance, the existence of God. On the other hand, I do not think that unverifiable religious beliefs can stand against the findings of the reason within the field in which human reasoning powers are effective. So if belief, in the religious meaning of the word, were to commit one to holding that the reason could and should be overriden on its own ground by an irrational faith, then I should not be entitled to claim that I had again become a believer.

My present state of mind is, as far as I can judge, a common and characteristic one in the Western World in the generation into which I happen to have been born. It is an open state of mind, and the necessary price of this intellectual and moral boon is a partial break in one's vision and a certain tenseness in one's feelings. Finding myself in this situation does not strike me with dismay because I do not feel that it puts me out of tune with Reality insofar as I have any intimation of what Reality may be like. I am also not aggrieved because I feel grateful for the dark and broken glass that lets through to me my human glimmer of light. No doubt a perfect lens would be better to have than a cracked one, but it is very much better to have a cracked one than not to have any lens of any kind. The mind's cracked lens is mankind's greatest treasure.

*Gods of corn
and gods of battle
give proof that religion
has always been a part
of human culture.
... The historian's dilemma
and how Gibbon
fell into it*

Let us now see whether the modus vivendi that I have suggested will hold firm or will break down if we try to make it serve as common ground for the study of human affairs in the particularly controversial field of the study of religion. In setting out together on this inquiry, religious-minded and rationalist-minded explorers can at least find a common point of departure. For differ as they may and will in their interpretations of the significance of religious experience, they will agree that the practices, beliefs, and institutions to which this experience has given rise always have been, and still are, a most important element in human affairs. A test of whether they can travel together farther than just the first step will be their respective answers to two questions about the relation between religion and culture. If the rationalist asks the religious-minded party whether he agrees that religion is a part of human culture, this question, I should say, ought to receive the answer Yes. If the religious-minded party then asks the rationalist whether he agrees that religion is not only a part of culture but is also something more than that, the answer, I should say, ought again to be Yes.

Religion is certainly one of those parts of culture that have usually been closest to the heart of it and also most closely associated with other parts; and this generalization becomes more clearly valid the farther we look back into the past. In all societies down to the rise of the "higher religions" in and after the last millennium B.C., religion has been intimately connected not only with art but also with social structure, political organization, and economic activities. The connection with economics seems to have come earliest. Before Man had gained the upper hand over nonhuman nature, the elements in his environment, from which he was wresting a precarious livelihood, were the medium through which he felt himself to be in touch with the spiritual presences higher than himself, in whose existence and potency he believed. It has been only in societies in which a considerable, and influential, minority of the population has been living an urban life for a considerable time that the worship of gods manifest in nature has fallen into the background; and then, when Man has become confident enough in his own powers to begin to divest nature of her aura of divinity, he has come to find a more impressive manifestation of the godhead in his own

social organization and in the collective power which he has acquired through this. In this next stage, religion comes to be connected with politics more pronouncedly than with economics. The gods who now inspire the strongest feelings of awe, fear, and love are manifestations of divinity seen through the medium of states. The god of the city-state of Nippur or goddess of the city-state of Argos now overshadows the storm-god or the corn-goddess; and Athena holds her worshipers' allegiance as the divinity manifest in Athens rather than as the one manifest in the olive tree.

Eventually the advent of the higher religions brings with it a new vision of the transhuman spiritual presence. Whether this is experienced as being immanent or as being transcendent, as being personal or as being impersonal, in every mode it is now experienced direct, and not through either an economic or a political medium. But the higher religions have so far had to incorporate almost as much as they have been able to abolish in the traditions of the earlier religions that they have sought to supersede. In the annual cycle of the liturgy of the Christian Church as this is still observed in many of the Church's present branches, the underlying annual cycle of agricultural operations is manifest. The most conspicuous manifestation is in the thanksgiving service for the harvest. Again, when in a Christian place of worship a *Te Deum* is sung to celebrate the victory of one professedly Christian state in a battle with another, the god to whom the thanks are given is manifestly the "god of battles," who is the symbol of the collective power of a local political community rather than the One True God who, according to Christian doctrine, is the common god not only of all Christians but of all human beings and all other created things.

Once it has been agreed that religion has in the past been an important part of culture, the historian's personal bias becomes a factor in his treatment not only of religion but of all human affairs. Whether he be religious-minded or rationalist-minded, he must face the fact that some of the human objects of his study have been in the opposite camp. Up to the present this obstacle to full sympathetic understanding has been less formidable for the religious-minded student of human affairs than it has been for the rationalist simply because, up to date, the vast majority of human beings have been religious-minded. The rationalist-minded humanist has to study a world of men with whom he is out of sympathy, with the exception of a few kindred spirits that catch his eye here and there.

A classical example of the rationalist-minded observer's handicap is the limitation which this state of mind imposed on the achievements of so great a genius as Edward Gibbon. Gibbon's case is an outstanding one because he was a genius who was rationalist-minded to an almost naïvely unselfcritical degree and who chose for his field of study an epoch of history in which a temporary access of rationalism was engulfed by a resurgence of religious faith. In Gibbon's eyes the spirit of Hellenic rationalism was identical with the spirit of the Western rationalism of Gibbon's own day. It was the same intellectual light dispelling the same darkness of ignorance and superstition; and Gibbon's subject was the submergence of Hellenic rationalism by the rise of Christianity. He saw his theme as the story of a catastrophe.

In approaching his subject from this standpoint, Gibbon could hardly help seeing almost all the characters on his stage in one or other of the two roles of fool or knave. If they were not cheats, they must be dupes. *Ex hypothesi,* a rational human being could not really believe in religion, so if someone who was unmistakably rational professed to believe in it, he must be an impostor seeking to deceive his fellow man for his own self-interested purposes. Conversely, if someone was an unmistakably sincere believer, he must be an irrational fool. The psychological barrier that the relativity of Gibbon's outlook interposed between the historian and the great majority of the figures passing across his stage prevented Gibbon from entering into the true motives and feelings of many of these actors, and therefore also prevented him from gaining a really penetrating insight into the meaning of the play. Gibbon's failure in these two respects—and the two points are both crucial—strikingly illustrates the seriousness of the handicap imposed by relativity when this is not corrected by self-criticism; for Gibbon's mind was surely the most powerful and most lucid one that has appeared so far in the whole distinguished company of Western historians up to date.

*Like Spengler,
Toynbee starts out by
trying to fit religion
into his pattern of
human culture. The system
works for the older gods
and the earlier societies*

Having agreed that religion is a part of human culture, the rationalist-minded humanist may, however, go on to insist that religion is merely this and nothing more. Let us try the policy of treating religious practices and institutions simply as parts of the culture of some society or some community within a society that is not primarily, or at any rate not solely, religious in character. This policy seems to work so long as we are dealing with primitive societies and with civilizations of the first generation. In these societies, as we have seen already, religion is closely connected not only with art but with economics and, later on, with politics; and further inspection shows that religion also enters into almost every other kind of activity in which the participants in these societies engage: for instance, war, education, and recreation. These societies do seem to be highly integrated and more or less self-contained; and their religious horizon seems to coincide with their boundaries on other planes.

This is obvious in the case of the political divinities; their respective realms do not even embrace the whole of the society in which their worshipers participate. A political god's writ runs only within the frontiers of the local state whose collective power he or she symbolizes; and even in those rare cases in which a local state—say Babylon or the Thebaid or Rome—expands into a universal state, the realm of the presiding god or gods—Marduk or Amen or Dea Roma and Divus Caesar—expands only up to the limits of the worshipers' empire. It might seem, at first sight, as if the older gods, in whom the superhuman spiritual presences manifest themselves through the medium of nonhuman nature, must, like this medium, have a more or less world-wide range. Olives grow in other countries besides Attica; Mother Earth yields corn at other places besides Eleusis; and the sea has no bounds. So how can the Attic olive-goddess Athena and the Eleusinian Earth-goddess Demeter and the Corinthian sea-god Poseidon be merely local divinities? Demeter of Eleusis did, as a matter of fact, extend her realm beyond Eleusis and beyond Attica to embrace the whole Hellenic World; but in this she was exceptional. Local nature-gods, who reigned in principle wherever their natural media—sea, corn, olive trees, and so on—were to be found, were in fact conscripted by their local worshipers to concentrate their attention on meeting local economic needs. In fact, economic as well as political divinities were community-bound. There were as many of each of them as there were communities to require their services. Even the goddess whose medium was the boundless Earth was not allowed to be one and indivisible. Every economically autarkic territory had, under some name or other, a Demeter of its own.

So long as the horizon of religion is thus bounded by the borders of regional societies, or even by the frontiers of states into which such societies are divided up or unified politically, it remains possible to treat religion just as a part of culture and as nothing more. But the possibility of continuing to take this line becomes doubtful and disputable when the "higher religions" make their appearance.

Higher religions, as a class, may be defined by characteristics of theirs which are revolutionary new departures. They catch a new vision of the spiritual presences, higher than Man, in which these presences are no longer seen through the medium of human economic and political needs and activities. There is a disengagement of the transhuman spiritual presence—and, with It, of Its worshipers—from the highly integrated life of some particular local community, and this disengagement has the consequence that the presence's realm now comes to be thought of as being co-extensive, not with some local state or some regional civilization, but with the entire Universe, while Its worshipers come to feel themselves members of a church that, in principle and in intention, embraces all men.

When the transhuman spiritual presence is seen direct instead of through the medium of human social needs and activities, human beings who have attained this new vision will be impelled to act on it in two new ways. They will want to enter into a new association with each other, independent of their traditional social ties; and they will want to communicate to the rest of mankind the saving truth about Reality that has been revealed to, or been discovered by, the adherents of the new religion in their belief. The emergence of this impelling sense of mission, with nothing short of the whole World for its field, raises the question whether the histories and institutions of the higher religions can really be stowed, like those of older religions, within the frameworks of the histories and institutions of particular pre-existing societies of a kind that is not primarily religious. May it not be found that the higher religions must be treated as societies of a new species and must therefore be regarded as phenomena which cannot be dealt with in terms of any other species than their own if they are to be dealt with adequately —that is to say, intelligibly? This question can be brought into sharper focus. Can each of the higher religions be regarded as being one of the products and expressions of some particular civilization, and as being nothing more than that?

An orderly rationalist mind will be reluctant to be convinced that this question cannot be answered in the affirmative; for if it can be, without doing violence to the phenomena, this will be a victory for simplicity and for clarity. It will make for simplicity because it will allow the student of human affairs to go on dealing with human history, since the emergence of the earliest civilizations about five thousand years ago, in terms of a comparative study of this species of society and of this one only. The subsumption of higher religions under civilizations will also make for clarity because it will make it possible to go on treating religion simply as a part of human culture. The powerful appeal of this rational quest for clarity and simplicity got the better of me, for one, when I was working out the original plan for my study of history. I decided to try to bring the whole field of human affairs, since the appearance of the earliest civilizations, within the framework of a comparative study of civilizations. And, before I started to put this decision into action, I was reassured by the publication of the first volume of Spengler's work, in which I found that my own intended plan of operations had been anticipated, with apparently complete assurance, by an inquirer who was obviously a man of genius. The same plan of operations has since been followed by Philip Bagby in *Culture and History;* and I should guess that he, too, was attracted to it by the promise of clarity and simplicity that this plan appears to hold out before one has begun to put it to the test of applying it to the phenomena. This empirical test raises the question, Do the phenomena allow of this apparently clear and simple solution of the problem presented by the appearance of the higher religions?

As the faith of a "chosen people," Judaism remains rooted in the culture of its origin. Like Hinduism and Zoroastrianism, it forfeits its destiny as a universal religion

If we start by looking at the three oldest of the higher religions—Judaism, Zoroastrianism, and Hinduism—we may be inclined to judge that these can each be subsumed under a particular civilization more or less legitimately. It is true that all three, like other representatives of the new species of religion, conceive of the godhead as being sovereignly self-sufficient and omnipresent. Brahma, Ahura-Mazda, and Yahweh reign, each of them, over the whole of mankind and the whole of the Universe. They are not just the respective communal divinities of the Hindus, the Parsees, and the Jews. It is also true that the followers of all three religions have shown concern to propagate their faiths. The Jews converted to Judaism the royal family of the Kingdom of Adiabene (in what is now Iraqi Kurdistan) in the first century of the Christian Era, and the royal family of the Turkish Khazar horde, on the steppe between the Lower Volga and the Lower Don, in the eighth century; and in the fastnesses of the Caucasus and of the Semyen Mountains in Abyssinia, there are today highland clans professing the Jewish religion. Likewise, Zoroastrianism and Hinduism sought and made converts at certain times and places.

Yet none of these three religions ever took the new road decisively. In their conception of the role of Almighty God, their adherents became arrested in a state of double thinking which to Christian and Muslim minds seems paradoxically inconsistent. After they had come to think of God as the omnipresent lord of the Universe, they went on thinking of Him at the same time as still being the peculiar local god of the society or community in which He had originally been worshiped as such. Thus each of these three religions, in becoming a higher religion, still also continued to be a part of the integrated culture of a particular community or society; and it has never become feasible to be converted to the Jewish, the Zoroastrian, or the Hindu religion without at the same time having to become a naturalized member of Jewish, Zoroastrian, or Hindu society. Conversion to Judaism or Zoroastrianism has involved submission to a system of law in which religious observances are inextricably intertwined with what, to Christian and Muslim minds, would seem like purely secular regulations. Conversion to Hinduism has involved incorporation in a caste and submission to the restrictions that the Hindu caste system entails. This explains why conversions to these three religions have been rare, and why their adherents have been no more than halfhearted in their efforts to bring gentiles into their jealously guarded folds. The source of the perennial ill-feeling between Jews and gentiles, and of the tragedies and atrocities in which this ill-feeling has repeatedly come to a head, is the inability of both gentiles and Jews to tell whether being a Jew means being an adherent of a religion or whether it means being a partaker in the culture of a community that, even in dispersion, has retained its original ethnic character.

The question whether Judaism is part of the culture of a community or whether it is a religion that can be embraced by anyone, whatever his ancestral culture or his local nationality may be, is the question that was at issue in the first generation of Christianity between the Jewish Christian church and the gentile Christian church created by the missionary work of Saint Paul. And it is significant that the secession of the Christian Church from Jewry, which followed in spite of Paul's and Peter's unanimous desire to avoid the breach, was not the only case of its kind. Six hundred years later, another new religion inspired by Judaism, namely Islam, parted company with Jewry, as Christianity had done, on a mission to convert the gentiles to the saving truth which the Jews had been keeping to themselves, like the talent wrapped in a napkin and buried in the earth by the servant in one of Jesus' parables.

In the history of Zoroastrianism it has been the same story. During the age in which Zoroastrianism was the established national religion of the Sassanian Empire, Manichaeism seceded from it in the third century of the Christian Era and Mazdaism in the fifth century; and in the following age, when the Sassanian Empire, as well as half the Roman Empire, had been conquered by the Muslim Arabs, the new regime's Zoroastrian subjects in Iran were converted to Islam much more rapidly than were its Christian subjects in Iraq, Syria, and Egypt. In the history of Hinduism, Buddhism and Jainism seceded in the sixth century B.C.

These portentous secessions are evidence of an unresolved tension in the bosom of the Jewish, Zoroastrian, and Hindu societies between a will to transform the ancestral religion of one people into a religion for all men and a reluctance to cast before swine the pearls that were the spiritually privileged people's heirloom. The tension resulted in repeated secessions because, in each of these three cases, a people that had seen the vision of a higher religion could not bring itself to go the whole way either in accepting the consequences or in rejecting them. It shrank from paying the price of collective self-abnegation that has to be paid by a "chosen people" if they are to become the missionaries of a world-wide faith; yet at the same time it could never turn its back on this vision when once it had seen it. This infirmity—common to Judaism, Zoroastrianism, and Hinduism—of hovering on the borderline between two ideals makes it just possible for a systematist to treat each of these three religions as being no more than the religious component (or part of this) in the culture of one of the civilizations.

Christianity has survived the fall and rise of civilization. Like Buddhism and Islam, it resists the attempt to treat it as part of a human culture pattern

But is it possible to dispose of Islam, Christianity, and Buddhism in the same way? Spengler's and Bagby's system of cultural and social morphology takes for granted their thesis that each of the higher religions is wholly contained within one or another of the civilizations and that each of them is also wholly explicable in terms of its container-civilization. I took this line myself till I was pulled up short by the intractability, as I saw it, of the phenomena.

If Spengler and Bagby found themselves forced by the historical evidence to admit that one of the higher religions had, at one or another time and place, been in some relation with two or more civilizations without ever losing its own identity, they would then be bound to admit that this particular higher religion was not, after all, wholly contained in one single civilization and wholly explicable in terms of this. To vindicate the validity of their morphology they must demonstrate either that each of the higher religions has run its course, so far, within the channel of some single civilization's history; or, alternatively, that if a higher religion has apparently been in relations with more civilizations than one, this apparent historical datum is illusory. What has transcended the limits of a single civilization is merely a common name, with no common substance corresponding to it.

Thus we find Bagby following Spengler in treating Christianity in the Western World since the eleventh century of the Christian Era as being a different religion, in spite of the common label, from Christianity in the West before that date and from Christianity elsewhere down to the present day. This contention is surely a paradoxical one; for surely Christianity, in all its later forms, bears not only a common name but a common character impressed on it by the experiences and achievements of the Christian Church during the first four and a half centuries of its existence. This age—the age of the Apostles, Martyrs, Fathers, Anchorites, and Creeds—has manifestly been the formative one. Compared to the decisive developments that occurred within that period, all subsequent developments in Christianity as a whole or in any of its branches have been no more than minor variations on the original theme; but the manifest formative period of Christianity was over, and the distinctive character of Christianity was firmly set, more than five hundred years before the emergence of the Western Civilization according to Spengler's chronology, which Bagby adopts.

It is hardly possible to label the culture of the modern

West "Near Eastern." But, once it has been conceded that there are two different civilizations—first what Bagby labels a "Near Eastern" civilization and then a Western one—with which Christianity has been in relations, it must be argued, on Spengler's and Bagby's hypothesis, that there are two different Christianities—a separate religion to fit into each separate culture-frame. If this is not demonstrated, it will have to be admitted that Christianity has been in relations with two different civilizations with no change in its own identity; and this, in its turn, would mean that Christianity is a phenomenon which cannot be classified in terms of any particular civilization and which must therefore be a representative of some different species of society.

This last-mentioned alternative is, I myself believe, the correct conclusion to draw. I, too, originally tried to account for the higher religions simply in terms of the civilizations. I took my cue from the relations, as I interpreted them, between the Christian Church on the one side and the Hellenic, Byzantine, and Western civilizations on the other; and I took this set of relations as my "model" for interpreting the historical roles of other religions of the "higher" species.

Following my clue, I saw a higher religion as a mechanism by which the species of society called civilizations had provided for its own reproduction. I thought of higher religions as being "chrysalises" into which a disintegrating civilization entered in the last stage of its dissolution and from which a new civilization subsequently emerged. This view of the historical role of the higher religions was, I now think, a variation on the same fundamental error that I see in Spengler's and Bagby's view. It assumed that the higher religions were significant solely on account of their serviceableness to societies of a different kind from their own. Starting from my own taking-off point, I arrived at different findings from Spengler's and Bagby's over some points of detail. Instead of thinking that a higher religion always originated inside some single civilization, I thought that it always originated from an encounter between two civilizations or more, and that this encounter was always preceded by the breakdown and disintegration of at least one of the parties to it. One of the outward visible signs of social breakdown, as I saw it, was the spiritual secession of a proletariat from a ruling minority that could no longer maintain its dominant position by anything better than sheer force. I saw that in several cases the seceding minority met and mingled with fellow proletarians seceding from some other civilization, and I thought that higher religions were the offspring of encounters between civilizations at this social level. Seeing Christianity as the offspring of an encounter between the Hellenic and the Syriac Civilization, and judging that both civilizations were in disintegration when this happened, I applied the same formula rightly, perhaps, to the history of the Mahayanian form of Buddhism, and wrongly, as I am now convinced, to the history of the

worship of Osiris—to take, as illustrations, two cases out of a number that I tried to identify, analyze, and interpret. These differences of detail do not acquit me from the charge that in the earlier stages of my inquiry I was making the mistake into which, as I now see it, Spengler and Bagby, too, have fallen. The view that I now hold has been exactly expressed by Christopher Dawson:

"The great civilizations of the World do not produce the great religions as a kind of cultural by-product; in a very real sense, the great religions are the foundations on which the great civilizations rest . . . We shall never create a living religion merely as a means to an end."

Religious faith comes by grace, not by will. Religion cannot be called to heel, like a dog, to suit human convenience.

At certain times and places, living religions have been tempted or driven into serving as a means to nonreligious ends; but to take these episodes of their history as their *raison d'être*, as I have done in the past, is to misunderstand and misinterpret their mission. So, far from this service of secular purposes being a fulfillment of their mission, it is a diversion from it; and whenever a higher religion has allowed itself to be shunted into this sidetrack, there has always been a spiritual-minded minority among its adherents who have remained faithful to their religion's true purpose. When in the Roman Empire the Christian Church was not only granted toleration but was made virtually a department of state, the anchorites withdrew into the Desert, and the Donatists, Nestorians, and Monophysites successively seceded from a church which the Monophysites branded as "Imperialist" (Melchite).

The higher religions are bound always to strive to keep themselves disengaged from secular social and cultural trammels because this is an indispensable condition for the fulfillment of their true mission. This mission is not concerned directly with human beings' social or cultural relations with each other: its concern is the relation between each individual human being and the transhuman spiritual presence, of which the higher religions offer a new vision. We may believe that this vision is an hallucination, or we may believe that it is a revelation or discovery of Reality; our choice between these two interpretations of the phenomena will be determined by, and relative to, our fundamental presuppositions. But whichever interpretation we adopt, we can perhaps agree upon accepting four propositions about the phenomena themselves. The first of these surely uncontroversial propositions is that the believers in the higher religions are convinced that their religious experience is not illusory. The second is that this conviction, whether justified or not, has given them the faith to move mountains. The third proposition is that the deeds which the adherents of the higher religions have done, and the institutions which they have built up, loom large in the panorama of human affairs since the date when religions of this kind first appeared on the scene. The fourth proposition—which has, I hope, been demonstrated more or less convincingly in these pages—is that in a study of human affairs the higher religions cannot be dealt with intelligibly simply as products or parts of particular civilizations. They require to be dealt with, at least on a par with civilizations and with pre-civilizational societies, as primary phenomena that cannot be reduced to terms of anything other than themselves.

*The historian ends up
as a "transrationalist,"
believing that there is a Reality
beyond reason but that
no one religion has a monopoly
of truth or salvation.
"Christ is Buddha"*

The unclosed rift between orthodox believers and unorthodox "transrationalists," of whom I am now one, is not, of course, the first schism that there has ever been within the ranks of those who do not find in rationalism a convincing explanation of Reality. There are also the schisms between the different orthodoxies themselves, and these go back to the first appearance of the higher religions on the scene. Each of the higher religions has always been intolerant of all the others, besides being intolerant of religions of the older "pagan" kind; and this, though tragic, is not surprising, for intolerance is the defect of the higher religions' virtue. The direct vision of Reality that each of them has caught is so much more convincing and inspiring than the older religions' vision of it that the adherents of each higher religion have jumped to the conclusion that their own religion is a unique discovery, or revelation, of absolute truth and a unique means of salvation. Only the adherents of higher religions of Indian origin have kept their minds open to the possibility that there may be more facets of truth and more ways of salvation than one. The reason why they have remained comparatively tolerant is that they have made less sharp a break than the higher religions of the Judaic groups have made with previous forms of religion; for the virtue of "pre-higher" religion's defects is its readiness to "live and let live."

It is, of course, impossible that each of the higher religions can be right in believing that it has a monopoly of truth and salvation; but it is not at all impossible that all of them should have found alternative roads to salvation and should have seen truth, "through a glass, darkly," in one or another of truth's different facets. This is what I myself have come to believe. This belief does not necessarily involve the further belief that all the higher religions have seen the truth in equal measure and have found roads to salvation that are equally good. Nevertheless, I fear that Dawson will have been right in his forecast that orthodox theologians would find my position unacceptable. A belief in the relative truth and relative saving-power of all the higher religions alike will seem tantamount to unbelief in the eyes of an orthodox believer in any one of them.

It is sad to find oneself at variance with fellow human beings with whom one believes—notwithstanding their contrary belief—that one is really in agreement over the heart of the matter at issue. But I am anchored in my present moorings by two convictions that will not let go of me. I am convinced that the spiritual presence that is higher than Man is merciful and compassionate in Its aspect in which It presents Itself to us as a person and in which we see It as God. And I am convinced that every human being is capable of catching a vision of the transhuman presence and of entering into communion with It, whether he finds It in Its personal aspect as Brahma or in Its impersonal aspect as Brahman or as Nirvana. Each of these two convictions can stand by itself; yet, though they are independent, they give each other mutual support, for each of them implies the other; so, if either of them is a true insight into Reality, the other cannot be a delusion. Together they give, for me, an assurance that the presence behind the phenomena is not capricious, and that the capacity to enter into communion with It is of the essence of human nature. I therefore believe that there never has been, and never will be, a "chosen" people or sangha or church invested with a monopoly of truth and salvation. Any such monopoly, if it were conceivable (and it is not conceivable to me), would be invidious both for the recipient and for the donor of the privilege. It would not be consonant either with Man's nature or with God's nature as I see them. And as long as I continue to see them as I do, I shall also continue, as far as I can foretell, to remain in the theological position in which I now find myself.

This stand of mine may put me out of communion with the orthodox adherents of each of the higher religions (at any rate, each of those in the Judaic group). It lies with the orthodox, not with me, to decide whether, in their eyes, I am within their pale or am beyond it. But it lies with me, not with them, to feel the feelings that I, too, feel towards those sublime figures that are revered and adored by me as well as by their orthodox followers or worshipers. No human writ of excommunication can come between those saviours and me. My knee bows, like every Christian's knee, at the deed of self-sacrifice, done for love of us men and for our salvation, that is recited by Saint Paul to the Philippians. For me, the doer of this deed is one presence in more than one epiphany. It is Christ, and because it is Christ, it is also the Buddha and the bodhisattvas.

THE
ART
OF
THE
HOAX

DRAWINGS BY DAVID LEVINE

Inspired by a pure love of mischief,

the perfect hoax may become

an elegant instrument of social satire

By GILBERT HIGHET

lue, gold, white, gold, and blue. Blue skies, golden sun, white foam flying; white uniforms, gold epaulets, and the solid, confident blue of the Royal Navy. Above, bright strings of signal flags snapping in the breeze: the pennant of an admiral and the white ensign of the Royal Navy. Below, the British Channel Fleet in review order showing its full strength in the year 1910. It lay at anchor at Weymouth, a disciplined mass of huge gray ships, their paint spotless, their decks blinding, their brass-work dazzling: little dispatch boats weaving a net of white curving wakes across the blue among them. On the Admiral's quarter-deck, one discordant note to spoil the splendid harmony: a small group of foreigners, with black faces and cocoa beards and huge rolling yellow eyes, speaking an ugly and incomprehensible language, and sloppily dressed in robes and turbans which might be intended to be formal but which looked like old curtains and carpets and rugs and towels. The men and their gabble and their robes were a stain on the trim *Dreadnought*. The stain was, no doubt, inevitable, but it was temporary. It would remove itself in a few hours. Meanwhile it had to be endured. It was an emperor, with his suite. The emperor was the guest of the Foreign Office; his realm, Abyssinia, was a strategically interesting and potentially rich area in northeastern Africa, and so a visit to the Channel Fleet had been specially arranged for the Emperor of Abyssinia and his suite.

The battleship was dressed. The crew was mustered. The guard of honor—Royal Marines in red and blue parade uniforms—presented arms and was inspected by His Majesty. The band struck up a ceremonial march. The great guns were raised and lowered and turned, as though the *Dreadnought* were a powerful half-tamed animal showing its teeth and claws, ready for a fight to the death. The Emperor watched and remained impassive. His courtiers and attendants rolled their liquid amber eyes and wagged their beards in astonishment. "Entaqui, mahai, kustufani!" they said to one another; and every moment they looked more frightened, more and more deeply impressed.

Nothing ruffles the courtesy of the Royal Navy. Although neither he nor any of his staff could speak Amharic, the Admiral still contrived to converse cordially and diplomatically with the Emperor. Through an interpreter whom His Majesty had brought with him—an immensely tall and gawky German who appeared to be about to despair of his all but impossible task—the Admiral explained that the Marines

who wore red were gunners and the Marines who wore blue were foot soldiers. The interpreter assimilated this information. He thought for a while, moving his lips, and then he explained. "Tahli bussor ahbat tahl aesque miss," he said, and the Emperor nodded gravely. "Erraema, fleet use, fert queré fert, queso ror!" Enlightenment dawned in the hooded eyes of the monarch. He gazed at the Marine guard. It was clear that the distinctive hues of their uniforms had already caught his eye; and now he realized that it was not merely a whim or a phenomenon of Western barbarism. It had a meaning. He nodded and slowly, meditatively belched. It was a sign of profound satisfaction.

At length, after several hours of slow progress through the inwards of H.M.S. *Dreadnought*, the imperial visit drew to a close. Would His Majesty care to take lunch with the Admiral and his senior officers? Alas, no. It was quite impossible. His Majesty's religious beliefs prevented him from touching any food whatever which had not been prepared in the strictest accordance with ancestral ritual. With expressions of gratitude for the Admiral's courtesy, the monarch and his suite took their leave. Boatswains' pipes split the air. The Marine guard presented arms. The ship's band, having been unable to find the national anthem of Abyssinia, broke into the national anthem of Zanzibar. The Admiral's launch accepted its august crew and sped towards shore. Only one contretemps marred the final minutes of the imperial visit. As the launch approached Weymouth dock, a picket boat crossed its bow. It is of course the grossest discourtesy to cross the bow of a vessel carrying royalty, and the young officer in command ought to have known that, for he had some connections with royalty, being called Battenberg (later Mountbatten); but he was summoned by his captain and severely reprimanded. Otherwise, the visit was successfully concluded. The Emperor's attendants tipped the launch's crew magnificently and offered a gorgeous decoration to its young commander, which he dutifully declined as against naval etiquette; and then the entire party disappeared into the imperial compartment on the London train, smiling ivory smiles and saying to one another, "Heia age! rumpe moras!"

The Admiral and his staff sat down to dinner in the wardroom, congratulating themselves on having got through a rather sticky afternoon without too much bobbery. Speeding back to London, the Emperor and his aides were also felicitating one another. They had found the visit a complete success. At times they had almost despaired of carrying it

Elegant Hoaxer: Hugh Troy

The people next door were due home after spending six months in Europe. Troy wired two barrels of ripe apples onto their cherry tree; and they called in half the town to look at the miracle of a cherry tree bearing apples, before it occurred to them to inspect the branches. Everything changes when you go abroad.

Whenever he got a wrong-number call, he would never hang up but always accepted it with great conviction. Once he got a series of calls intended for a bookmaker; he invented fictitious horses, quoted startling odds, and accepted, with remarkable alacrity, dangerous bets.

He and his brother, when young, had to stay with an aged and rather tedious grandmother for two months every summer. They made the time pass by mixing up the calendar. First, they got grandma a day behind, so that she believed Friday was Thursday, and then, stage by stage, they convinced her that Wednesday was really Sunday. On Wednesday Troy would bring out the Sunday papers (which he had kept hidden for four days), the maid would cook a special chicken dinner, and grandma would lead the little household in prayer.

One of his most famous hoaxes has the simplicity and charm of a Capablanca chess ending. A professor at Cornell used to take off his overshoes and leave them at the door of the lecture hall. During one lecture, Troy painted them white, to look like large feet, with big toes and toenails. Then he coated them with lampblack. The professor put them on at the end of the lecture and walked back across the campus; as the lampblack washed off, he appeared to be paddling happily home in huge bare feet.

through, but now that it was over they could scarcely believe that they had managed it all with such superb aplomb, such resolute refusal to falter before the power and prestige of the Navy, and such amazing fluency in the Ethiopian language. For the Admiral and his officers it had been a diplomatic ordeal. For the Emperor and his suite it had been a magnificent hoax. They were not Ethiopians. They were not even foreigners. They were all English. The Emperor of Abyssinia was a handsome young man called Anthony Buxton. His escort, putatively from the Foreign Office, was the greatest of modern English jokers, Horace de Vere Cole, wearing a superbly diplomatic morning coat and top hat. His interpreter, Kauffmann, was a Bloomsbury intellectual who had been a little embarrassed on the quarter-deck when he thought that his six-foot-five-inch stature and unmistakable features would surely be recognized by various friends and relatives among the *Dreadnought*'s crew. Cole's suite were all young men with good family connections and a strong

sense of humor—except one, who was a girl. They knew her as the interpreter's sister, Virginia Stephen; the world knew her later as Virginia Woolf.

It had been easy, unexpectedly easy, for Cole and his friends to be received by the Admiral. They had simply sent him a telegram warning him that the Emperor was arriving, and appended to it the name of the head of the Foreign Office. Their costumes had been rented from the best London theatrical costumer, Clarksons; and Clarkson himself had secured their beards and stained their faces. The language had been a serious problem. The ever inventive Cole had tried to teach "Kauffmann" some words of Swahili, in the hope that they could be extrapolated; but poor Kauffmann, when he had to explain why some Marines wore red and others blue, was forced to fall back on the only foreign language he knew really well. At school he had learned many hundreds of lines of Homer and Vergil by heart, and at the crisis of the Marines' uniforms, he began, slightly distorting and misplacing the syllables and accents, the pathetic description of Dido's desperate pleas to the lover who is deserting her:

*Talibus orabat talesque
miserrima fletus fertque
refertque soror. . . .*

Surely that was the perfect hoax, unique and incomparable? Probably; yet consider.

In the years before 1914, if there was one single military force which was prouder than the British Royal Navy, it was undoubtedly the German army. Its devotion to duty was ascetic. Its officers were aristocrats by birth, by selection, by training, and even by appearance. Its ambitions embraced and dominated the entire world. No one could despise it, and woe to that man who dared to ridicule it. And yet not only the German army but the German Reich and the hard, exact, cold bureaucracy which supported it were shown to be obtuse, mechanical, and absurd. They were converted briefly into the laughingstock of Europe, not by a humiliating defeat, nor by a painful scandal like the Dreyfus case, nor even by a joke like the *Dreadnought* hoax, but by an act of desperation committed by a petty crook who for one day became a genius.

In the autumn of 1906 the township of Köpenick, an ancient and peaceful foundation which had become a suburb of Berlin, was digesting its lunch and looking forward to its dinner. Two squads of German soldiers, marching smartly through its streets, did not disturb it. On the contrary, they reassured it, as a visible symbol of German might and German discipline. The Captain marching at their head, with his spiked helmet, his long field-gray overcoat, his heavy saber, and his air of high resolve, recalled the military efficiency of General von Moltke and the personal majesty of the Kaiser Wilhelm II. Even when the soldiers, with fixed bayonets, took up their positions in front of the Town Hall, even when the Captain posted a local policeman at its door and strode inside, the citizens of Köpenick were not alarmed: they were only curious and perhaps a little anxious in case, among the innumerable regulations and ordinances of the new Germany, they had transgressed (through oversight, not through failure of will power, still less through contumacy) one of them. Slowly, buttoning their waistcoats and brushing their mustaches, they began to gather before the Town Hall, gazing with respect and admiration at the impassive faces and heavy uniforms and glistening bayonets of the guard.

Meanwhile the Captain, followed by six grenadiers and a fusilier, mounted the staircase. He went first to the office of the Secretary.

"You are the Secretary of the Town Council?"

"Yes, Captain."

"Prepare yourself. You are being sent to Berlin."

"Very good, Captain."

Next, he went to the office of His Honor, the Mayor.

"You are the Mayor of Köpenick?"

"Yes, Captain."

"Prepare yourself. You are being sent to Berlin."

"Captain, may one enquire why?"

"I do not know. It is not part of my mission."

"Very good, Captain."

Next, he went to the office of the Chief of Police. The Chief of Police was snoozing deliciously in his chair, enjoying the peristaltic motion of his prandial pork and potatoes. Here the Captain really made his authority felt. Hastily buttoning his uniform, the Chief of Police was harshly reprimanded for dereliction of duty and sent home to take a bath which would clear his fat, dirty, sleepy, louse-ridden head.

Finally, he went to the office of the Town Treasurer.

"Clear your accounts and close your books. You are being sent to Berlin."

"Very good, Captain. I have here the sum of four thousand marks which has been paid in today, and which I have not yet entered. Will the Captain take charge of them, and give me a receipt?"

"Certainly."

"Here in the safe there are an additional two million marks. Will the Captain assume the responsibility for these also?"

For a moment the Captain seemed to interrogate himself. Then, with military promptness and the assurance which comes of long training, he decided.

"Not necessary. Close the safe. Take the key."

Signing the receipt, the Captain thrust the four thousand marks into his overcoat pocket and left the Treasurer to

"For everything that happens I am responsible"

make his preparations. Outside, a crowd of officials had gathered. All wanted answers to their questions, decisions on outstanding problems, clear, firm, authoritative guidance. In a few sentences the Captain resolved all their anxieties and gave them a final encouragement.

"The administration of this town is now in my hands. For everything that happens, I am responsible."

With relief and with admiration, they bowed and parted as the Captain moved to the door of the Town Hall. He returned the salutes of the policeman and the rigid military guard standing outside and strode away. Ten minutes later he was on the suburban train for Berlin. An hour later he was sitting in a café, wearing ordinary civilian clothes, drinking a glass of blond beer, and waiting for the papers to come out with the news from Köpenick.

He was not a Captain. He had never been in the army. He was an ex-convict named Wilhelm Voigt, who was approaching sixty years of age and had spent about half his life in prison. When Voigt worked, he was a shoe machinist; but because of his prison record, which had begun in his poverty-stricken youth, he could never find or keep settled employment. The efficient and ruthless German police were constantly making inquiries about him, checking his papers, and asking him to move on, from one city to another, from one state to another, until at last he determined to leave Germany altogether and settle in Austria or some other more peaceful, less interfering country. But to leave Germany, he

needed a passport. An ex-convict would never be given a passport. How could Voigt ever obtain one? Never by entreaty, only by authority. What authority did all Germans recognize? That of the army, the uniform, the spiked helmet, the air of command, and the squad of armed automata. Therefore Voigt procured a uniform and took command of the first squad of soldiers he met in the street; and the rest followed with elegant, drill-like precision. He made only one mistake: he went to Köpenick because he thought it was an efficient little town which would have every kind of blank document in its Town Hall—so that he need only get rid of the top officials on some pretext and then make out his own passport. It was inside the Town Hall that he realized his blunder. He had not underestimated the obedience and naïveté of German officials, but he had forgotten their passion for complexity and departmentalization. Passports were not issued by the police offices of towns and cities but by the police offices of administrative districts, and Köpenick was not the capital of an administrative district. Poor Voigt pocketed his four thousand marks (at least they would be eating-money), ignored the two million marks (which would have sent him to jail for the rest of his life), and vanished.

(By the way, do you notice anything familiar in the story? The poverty-stricken youth, with the long years in prison, the loneliness? The bold assumption of power without training? The rapid and summary abrogation of all civil authority? The hypnotic domination of long-experienced and le-

After the training he became Montgomery

gally appointed officials? The superb arrogance of the ultimate declaration: "For everything that happens, I am responsible?" Yes, the Captain of Köpenick was the immediate predecessor of Adolf Hitler.)

Wilhelm Voigt was soon arrested. Another ex-convict remembered hearing him say, in prison, "You can always get what you want in Germany by picking up a few soldiers in the street and requisitioning it." He was tried, and found guilty of fraud, impersonation, larceny, etc., and sentenced to four years in prison; but he was set free on the personal orders of His Imperial Majesty Kaiser Wilhelm II. We can scarcely imagine that His Majesty wished to confer an imperial favor on the man who had successfully mimicked one of his own officers and bamboozled several hundreds of his own subjects. Either he felt that Voigt, after nearly thirty years in jail, was not quite sane; or else he heard the waves of laughter which were wafted into Germany on every breeze, realized that the Captain of Köpenick had made the German army and German officialdom ridiculous, and determined, instead of being vindictive, to be magnanimous. Within Germany, Voigt's act was a complex of crimes. Outside Germany, it appeared to be a hoax. Which was it?

n 1944 an elderly British lieutenant called Clifton James, who had been a rather unsuccessful actor before the war, was picked out of a routine job in the desk-bound Army Pay Corps and given a special mission. He was to impersonate Field Marshal Viscount Montgomery. Physically, he looked very like his model: spare frame, keen birdlike face, brisk nervous manner. Spiritually, he was almost the exact reverse of that mystical martinet. But he was shown many motion pictures of Montgomery; he was seconded to Montgomery's personal staff in order to register the timbres of Montgomery's voice and observe his mannerisms; he was trained to fly without being airsick; he was fitted with a replica of Montgomery's highly individual uniform—beret, medal-ribbons, gold chain across the chest, and all—and finally he talked for some time with Montgomery himself, face to face. After this training, he was briefed, and he became Montgomery. First, he was flown out to Gibraltar, where he was received by the Governor with a guard of honor and closely observed by a number of German agents using Spanish cover. He then proceeded to Allied headquarters in North Africa, where he was seen in public for an entire week. Then he returned to Britain in utter secrecy and vanished. This impersonation was so successful that it deceived Admiral Canaris and his German intelligence staff. It was one element in the enormous and multiplex deception worked out by Allied intelligence officers in order to conceal from the Germans the time and place of the main D-day

Trenchant Hoaxes

Tchaikovsky's dramatic overture *1812* is a musical portrayal of Napoleon's invasion of Russia. The conflict is depicted by the counterpoint of French and Russian songs, with the "Marseillaise," at the end, overborne by the powerful strains of the Czarist hymn "God the All-Terrible." The hymn swells up louder and louder, fills the auditorium, blares to a triumphal climax, and then a salvo of artillery booms out. (Tchaikovsky meant the overture to be performed in the open air, with a real battery of guns firing blanks at the end.) At a performance of *1812* in Rochester, New York, in 1952, the orchestra built up its climax, the off-stage cannon boomed out a tremendous boom, and then, as the echoes were about to die away, from the roof of the auditorium there floated down a cloud of white duck feathers.

A man called Partridge annoyed Jonathan Swift by publishing almanacs full of prognostications for each coming year, which were, in Swift's eyes, tainted by Whig propaganda. Swift then issued a rival almanac forecasting the exact day, hour, and cause of Partridge's death—in March of the coming year; he then followed this up by an eyewitness account of the death scene and a funeral elegy. Partridge protested and even advertised in the newspapers that he was still alive; but no one would believe him. He had ceased to exist.

For many years a thin nervous intellectual called Ferdinand Lop was the perpetual candidate for the Presidency of France. He had no supporters except the students of the Sorbonne. To their warm applause he issued bold manifestoes saying how he would reform France when he came to power. With their shouted support, he denounced all other candidates as lacking in true idealism. The students were the mainstay of his party, which they called the Front Lopulaire; they defended him against the police, whom they called the Anti-Lops; and they sang a special campaign song for him to the tune of "The Stars and Stripes Forever": "Lop, Lop, Lop Lop Lop, Lop Lop Lop! Lop Lop Lop, Lop Lop Lop, Lop Lop LOP Lop!" Their reform program, called Lopeotherapy, included such radical measures as the elimination of poverty after 10 P.M., the nationalization of brothels, and the rebuilding of Paris in the country, where the air is fresher.

Horace de Vere Cole once took every seat in the stalls at a pretentious and terrible play and gave tickets to many acquaintances. The performance was wrecked, because as soon as the lights went up, the circles and the gallery saw one short and expressive word spelled out by the bald heads of strategically placed men in the stalls.

landings and, in particular, to make them believe that a massive blow, under Montgomery's command, would soon be delivered across the Mediterranean at southern France. This, like the rest of the magnificent D-day deception, was brilliantly successful. Was it a hoax?

Now, it is here that most books on famous hoaxes and famous hoaxers fail. A hoax is not an exaggeration or a lie told and acted for profit. A hoax is an exaggeration or a lie told and acted for amusement, for the sake of sheer mischief, for the sake of art. There is a fine anthology of swindles collected by Professor Curtis MacDougall, recently published in a second edition (*Hoaxes,* Dover Publications, 1958); but although it is rich in material, it spoils the appreciation of a delicate art by confusing elegant hoaxes with vulgar frauds and grimly serious deceptions. What connection is there between a vicious propaganda fabrication such as the *Protocols of the Elders of Zion,* a greedy series of forgeries like those seen in the career of Ivar Kreuger, and a neat, farcical, and virtually harmless mystification, as when Hugh Troy and a few friends dug up Fifth Avenue at Fifty-fourth Street and left the hole surrounded by signs saying MEN AT WORK.

It is the purpose and the effect that distinguish a hoax from other forms of deception. The swindler wants to get something. The hoaxer wants to create a work of art. The swindler wants either money, or power, or prestige, or revenge. The hoaxer wants to comment, to criticize, or to re-interpret. The swindler is a thief. The hoaxer is a satirist.

Now, look at the three impersonations again. When Lieutenant James pretended to be Field Marshal Montgomery, he was in deadly earnest. If he succeeded, his deception would help to save the lives of thousands of Allied soldiers; and we now know that all phases of the grand deception succeeded. When Hannibal drove a huge cattle herd along an Italian mountainside, with burning torches tied to their horns, to convince the Romans that his entire army was on the move, he was not hoaxing them; nor were the Japanese hoaxing when in the midst of diplomatic discussions and without a declaration of war, they attacked the United States fleet in Pearl Harbor.

The case of the Captain of Köpenick is more complex. The German army, administration, and police took his deception very seriously. But for the rest of the world, to whom it displayed in full bloom certain German characteristics which members of other nations find both absurd and repellent, it was a hoax. In effect it was the equivalent of a satire on German authoritarianism, German militarism, German accuracy, and the awful quality which the Germans believe to be unflinching loyalty but others call porcine obtuseness.

And what of the Emperor of Abyssinia and his visit to the British Channel Fleet? We might put it down simply as a prank, like putting a cow in the college chapel or giving a man the number of the zoo and telling him to call Mr. Wolf. But in fact it went deeper. The Admiral and his officers were derided for being taken in. When they went ashore, small boys followed them, shouting Abyssinian words such as "Bunga, bunga!" Questions were asked in Parliament. The entire thing had started as an attempt by one young British officer to pull the leg of another (the chief of the Admiral's staff); but it developed into a first-class satire. It exposed the uncritical readiness of the British government and of the Royal Navy to entertain any odd-looking foreigner without inquiring closely into his character and background and to do him the honors so thoroughly that he went away awed and happy and pro-British. That kind of diplomatic courtesy helped to build up an enormous empire and to keep many spheres of influence in orbit. The *Dreadnought* hoax was a mocking exposure of its shallowness and insincerity. Thus, the silly little blackface impersonation by half a dozen unemployed youngsters proved to be a satire on the entire British imperial system.

In drawing and painting, a hoax corresponds to caricature; in music, literature, and drama, to parody. What the "Emperor of Abyssinia" and his suite did to the Royal Navy with their official visit, Gilbert and Sullivan had done some years earlier with *H.M.S. Pinafore.* (It looks and sounds innocuous enough nowadays, dear old *Pinafore*; but when it was produced, its satire was felt to be so acid that Disraeli himself said it "made him quite sick" with mortification.)

Artists are not concerned with gaining power or making money. They are trying to interpret the world. Some see it and show it as tragic, some as comic, some as romantic or fantastic. But some see it as pretentious, ridiculous, occasionally repulsive: these are the satirists. With all the pomp and circumstance of an epic poet, Juvenal describes the cruel and foolish Emperor Domitian convoking an emergency meeting of his cabinet to determine how to cook a vast circular turbot, too big for any of the imperial pots. In a single black-and-white drawing, the British cartoonist David Low shows a little man with a ridiculous mustache and a railway official's uniform defying the Creator of the universe and threatening to destroy mankind. Using all the resources of a full orchestra, Ernst von Dohnanyi builds up an atmosphere full of hideous menace: vast blocks of sound move through the air as though some unchallengeable portent were being brought to birth, cellos groan and trombones roar like beasts of the primeval slime, the music swells to a fearful climax and falls silent. Then, with one finger, the pianist plays "Baa, baa, black sheep, have you any wool?"

It is in this realm of art, the only realm which combines the sublime and the ridiculous, that the hoax belongs. When Horace de Vere Cole strewed horse droppings (procured with considerable difficulty and expense from mainland Italy) about the center of that horseless city, Venice, and then watched the Venetians gazing with a wild surmise first at the pavement of the Piazza di San Marco and then at the sky above, where nothing has yet been seen to fly but pigeons and airplanes, he was enjoying the purest pleasure of art—which combines criticism, creation, and appreciation.

HOMER'S AGE OF HEROES

The classical Greeks knew it only by legend.

But modern scholars have found at

Mycenae the capital city of the lost civilization

that inspired the *Iliad* and the *Odyssey*

By C. M. BOWRA

In the last hundred and fifty years, scholars have done an enormous amount of work on the Homeric poems in their desire to find out when and how they were composed and what truth, if any, lies behind their stories. At times the critically minded might well ask to what end all this work was leading. The bits of the puzzle did not seem to fit; there was fierce disagreement on most fundamental points. But slowly and quietly, despite many false starts, progress has been made. The bits are coming together, and we can see the general pattern. Archaeology has brought the

NATIONAL MUSEUM, ATHENS; HIRMER VERLAG, MUNICH

Trojan War back from legend to history; the comparative study of oral epics has shown how Homer must really have worked; the discovery and decipherment of documents from the Greek past of 1200 B.C. have thrown unexpected lights into what seemed to be a lost world. The inspiration of a few men of genius and the solid support of many hard-working inquirers have changed the whole character of Homeric studies, and we can now relate Homer to his historical background and see how he worked and what he worked on.

The classical Greeks believed that at a period in the past, which our system of chronology would place from about 1400 to about 1200 B.C., their ancestors had been a race of super-men, of heroes, who were endowed physically and mentally beyond the common lot and who lived for action and the glory which it brings, especially through prowess in battle. Such a belief in a heroic past is to be found in many peoples, and for parallels we need look no further than the great Germanic migrations from the fourth to the sixth century A.D. or to the cycles of high adventure which the French connect with Charlemagne in the ninth century, or the Russians with

With a shower of spears and arrows Homeric warriors meet the charging lion on this bronze dagger found in a tomb at Mycenae. To the ancient Greeks, proud of their bravery and physical perfection, lion hunting was a sport—as well as a defense of their homes and flocks. Homer compares the clash of Trojan and Greek on the battlefield to mountain lions who "depopulate the stalls and waste the fold." This dagger, finely inlaid with gold and silver, bears out Homer's description of the huge body shields, some in figure-eight shape, which warriors of both armies carried on the battlefield of Troy.

MUSEUM OF FINE ARTS, BOSTON BETTMANN ARCHIVE

Homer   *Schliemann*   *Ventris*

Vladimir Monomakh of Kiev in the twelfth century, or the Yugoslavs with the fall of the old Serbian kingdom to the Turks at the battle of Kosovo in 1389. With such beliefs the Greek tradition of a noble past has much in common, and like them, it found its expression in heroic, narrative song. From what must once have been a vast mass of songs, we have only the *Iliad* and the *Odyssey*, which the Greeks, without hesitation, ascribed to Homer. In all their pristine strength and splendor these epics stand at the dawn of European literature as its first and in some ways its most remarkable achievement.

The *Iliad* and the *Odyssey* survive in isolation. Of other poems resembling them we have only a few stray lines, and of Homer himself we know next to nothing. He says not a word about himself, offers no personal judgments, and hardly ever speaks, even in the first person. External traditions about him are late, contradictory, and untrustworthy. Where all is darkness it is not surprising that some scholars have decided that he did not exist or at least did not compose the two poems, and many alternatives have been sought to what is regarded as the uncritical gullibility of the Greeks about him. The case for some kind of multiple authorship has appealed to many whose standards of literary criticism come from books composed in conditions very unlike those of the Homeric poems and who are unable to understand that in the course of centuries literature has changed its habits. For some one hundred and fifty years the Homeric poems have been carved into pieces by minute analysis and explained variously as combinations of single short lays, or expansions of original, basic poems, or ingenious transformations of poems dealing with quite different subjects. Yet all this labor has led to no single point of agreement. Each analyst believes he has found the solution, but he has no disciples. Something seems to have gone wrong, and we can in fact see what it is.

The fundamental error of the analytical method is that it treats the Homeric poems as if, like modern books, they were written to be read. They belong to a different, much older art. They were not written but recited, not read but heard, and the difference accounts for the peculiarities which have troubled modern scholars but did not trouble the Greeks. Before the invention of writing, all poetry was recited or sung, and the practice still flourishes in many regions where not everyone is literate, or books are confined to limited, special fields like law and theology, or recitation is still enjoyed for its own sake as a dignified and agreeable pastime.

The oral poet works quite differently from the poet who writes. Recitation is his only means of making his work known, and his first duty is to keep his audience's attention at all costs. If he bores or confuses them, he loses their interest and, with it, his source of livelihood. His technique, which comes from generations of practiced bards, tells him what to do. Above all he must not allow his story to become too complicated; he must deal with one and only one thing at a time, with all the clarity and firmness of outline of which he is capable. This means that he sacrifices much that the writer of books thinks indispensable. In oral art the moment a theme has done its task it is dismissed without ado, and no attempt is made to tidy the loose threads. The need to stress the special character of each dramatic occasion may lead to inconsistencies with what is said elsewhere. A long poem, whose performance may last for several days, may be loose in construction just because each episode must be complete in itself. A passage which performs one task in one place may be repeated word for word in another place to perform a slightly different task. The audience does not know what it is to turn over pages to see if everything fits exactly, and it is content with the fleeting situation as the spoken word reveals it. Oral poetry has its own rules, which are well known to us from a large mass of poems collected from many parts of the world where the art is still vigorous and popular. It is by the standards of this art that Homer must be interpreted and judged.

EMMETT L. BENNETT

Our knowledge of Mycenaean civilization springs in large measure from the work of the three men on the opposite page: the ancient poet and two amateur archaeologists. Homer's picture of an age of heroes, though accepted by the classical Greeks, had been generally dismissed as legend until Heinrich Schliemann, a German businessman, set out to prove its truth. In 1870 he uncovered the site of Troy and six years later began his excavation of the ruins of Mycenae. Schliemann's lead was followed up by Sir Arthur Evans on Crete and by Carl W. Blegen on the mainland. The next great breakthrough came in 1952, when Michael Ventris, a young English architect, deciphered the Linear B script found on tablets at Knossos, Pylos, and Mycenae. The tablets proved to be largely commercial records, but they show that the people spoke an archaic form of Greek and had a highly organized business and political life. The tablet shown at right is a record of a commercial transaction in wool.

Although the *Iliad* and the *Odyssey* were composed for recitation and show all its familiar marks, each has its own mastering design and its own kind of unity. In the *Iliad* the whole poem hangs upon the wrath of Achilles, and though other episodes are introduced on a generous scale to make it indeed a tale of Troy, it is the wrath which gives a unity to the whole. The last book picks up the themes of the first and tells the end of the wrath with which all the action began.

The *Odyssey* is composed in three movements: the first tells of the anarchic condition of Ithaca in the absence of Odysseus, the second of his many adventures between his departure from Troy and his final arrival on Ithaca, the third of his vengeance on Penelope's suitors after his arrival. In each movement the characters are admirably consistent, lifelike, and even at times complex. The rich, elaborate, and traditional language shows no real variation between one section and another, and the poetical vision is sustained throughout. Devices, such as similes or the repetition of conventional themes for the arming of warriors or the conduct of sacrifices or putting boats to sea, are managed with admirable judgment and made to provide variety just when it is needed. Both the *Iliad* and the *Odyssey* are clearly artistic wholes, and such interpolations as they may contain do not disturb the main pattern.

It does not necessarily follow that both poems are the work of the same poet. There are certainly differences between them, in temper, in language, in pace, in construction, and in outlook, but these are less than between *Romeo and Juliet* and *The Tempest* or between *Comus* and *Samson Agonistes*. All considered, the *Odyssey* looks very like a later work by the author of the *Iliad* and may have been intended to be in some sense a sequel to it. The poems were probably composed between 750 and 700 B.C., since such a date fits the latest datable details in them. They belong to a period from which almost no other literature survives, and their origin was certainly in Ionia on the eastern coast of the Aegean Sea.

There is no reason to think that their author's name was not Homer.

Between the events of which Homer tells and the lifetime of the poet himself there is a gap of some five hundred years. Another three centuries separate Homer from the classical Greeks of the Golden Age. These later Greeks believed that the main events of his poems were historically true, but of the poet's lost world they knew almost nothing—far less than we do today. It remained for modern research, moving on three main lines of discovery, to unearth an advanced civilization which corresponds in many respects to that of which Homer sang.

The first move came from archaeology, when in 1870 a retired German businessman, Heinrich Schliemann, who was obsessed by a passionate love of Homer, drove a deep trench into the traditional site of Troy near the southeastern shore of the Dardanelles. Three years later, after digging through many levels, he found what he thought to be the city of Priam and its treasure. But what he identified as Homeric Troy was, in fact, a city which flourished at least a thousand years earlier than any possible city of Priam, and at the end of his life Schliemann knew that he had not discovered what he sought. It fell to his successors, and especially to the University of Cincinnati expedition led by Professor Carl W. Blegen, to identify, in a higher level at the same site, the ruins of the city which must indeed be the Homeric Troy. Schliemann also attacked sites on the Greek mainland, notably at Mycenae, where he uncovered a royal graveyard where the bodies lay intact in all their gold masks and ornaments. The work his inspired insight inaugurated has been continued ever since, and each year it has added to our knowledge of this rich and spectacular past.

The heroic age of which Homer sang has its historical counterpart in this Mycenaean civilization, which had its beginnings in Crete, notably at Knossos. About 1450 B.C. Knossos waned and Mycenae waxed, developing its own new

TEXT CONTINUED ON PAGE 80

P-J. LAUNAY

The Lion Gate

Mycenae

The citadel of Mycenae, rising high above the Argive plain, was the stronghold, according to Homeric tradition, of Agamemnon, "king of men" and leader of the Greek armies against the Trojans. The walls are built of stones so huge that the Greeks of the classical age thought they must have been set in place by the Cyclopes. Actually the fortress palace was built between 1500 and 1300 B.C. and was destroyed by the "Dorian" invaders barely a century after Mycenaean power reached its apogee in the conquest of Troy. Mycenae had been a ruin for thirteen hundred years when the Greek traveler Pausanias saw it in the second century A.D. "There still remain," he wrote, "parts of the city wall, including the gate, upon which stand lions." The lions still stand guard, though headless, at the gate near the Grave Circle (right), which Pausanias thought to contain the tombs of Agamemnon and his family. Heinrich Schliemann, who excavated the tombs, likewise thought the skeletons he found were those of Homer's royal family, but modern archaeologists date them four centuries earlier. The golden treasure which the tombs yielded proves that even then Mycenae was a center of wealth, power, and artistic accomplishment unrivaled on the continent of Europe.

GEORGES VIOLLON, RAPHO

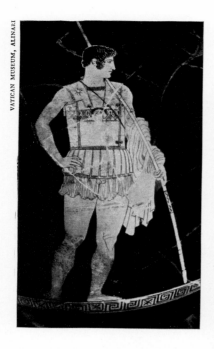

Homer's warriors were imagined by the Greeks of the classical age as handsome, noble figures like Achilles (above), shining in his famous armor adorned with the Medusa head. The ancient heroes' picture of themselves was far less flattering. On the Warrior Vase from Mycenae (right) the fighting men of 1200 B.C. are depicted as long-nosed, chinless types who seem more startled than eager to be marching to war.

TEXT CONTINUED FROM PAGE 77

movements in the fine arts and its own characteristic pattern of life. That it was fashioned for war is clear from the vast scale of its Cyclopean fortifications, from the rich variety of weapons found in its graves, from the many scenes of battle which its artists delighted to portray on gold or ivory or gems or pottery. Yet the Mycenaean world did not exist only for war. It made notable achievements in the fine arts, and its works and wares found markets in distant lands from the Adriatic to Syria. A power like this one was fully capable of maintaining a war such as that against Troy, and tradition may well be right in saying that the expedition was led by the king of Mycenae. But the Mycenaean civilization, which had many seats in the Peloponnesus and even northward as far as Thessaly, came to an abrupt and violent end about 1200 B.C., when its towns and citadels were destroyed and its material culture fell into rapid decay. The destroyers probably came from the northwest and, even if they were related racially to the Mycenaeans, were vastly inferior to them in culture. By 1200 the Dark Age of Greece begins.

A second, much less abundant source of information comes from Egyptian and Hittite records. The Egyptians were much troubled by the "Peoples of the Sea," and among these we may recognize two names which Homer uses for his Greeks—Achaeans and Danaans. The first took part in an attack against Egypt from the west about 1230 B.C. and were routed by Merneptah; the second peoples were among the confederates of a concerted invasion by land and sea about 1182 B.C. and were routed in the Nile Delta by Ramses III, who had reliefs of the battle carved on a pylon at his temple at Medinet Habu. The Hittite records, found in their ancient capital of Boghazköy, contain tantalizing references to the Ahhiyawans, who cannot be other than the Achaeans, and who played a considerable part in Hittite foreign affairs in the fourteenth and thirteenth centuries, first as allies and later as raiders by land and sea. They were classed as a great power; and in one document in particular the king of Ahhiyawa is mentioned as being the equal of the kings of the Hittites, the Egyptians, and the Babylonians, only to have his name

HARISSIADIS—NATIONAL MUSEUM, ATHENS

METROPOLITAN MUSEUM OF ART, ROGERS FUND 1907

"The rushing chariot and the bounding steed" of 1400 B.C. are depicted on the Mycenaean vase at left. By 450 B.C., when the Attic volute krater below was made, classical artists had added two horses and romanticized the legend of heroic times. But the design of the chariot remains basically the same in art as it did in fact for more than a thousand years.

A MYCENAEAN CHARIOT

AS SEEN BY A MYCENAEAN ARTIST (ABOVE)

. . . AND BY THE CLASSICAL GREEKS (RIGHT)

erased, as if in the interval he had forfeited his title to honor.

From the Egyptian and Hittite documents we get a clear enough picture of Achaeans, living probably on the Greek mainland but with outposts in Asia Minor and Cyprus, who through their ships pursued a policy of expansion toward the east and the southeast, aiming eventually at seizing land in Egypt. In such conditions an attack on Troy would have had its place; for Troy, which stood near the narrowest point of the crossing from Europe to Asia and seemed to have been a **tributary** of the Hittites, would have had to be captured before Asia Minor could be invaded from the northwest. For the Achaeans such a policy would have been almost a necessity, and we can understand why the Trojan War took place. The Achaeans, who are known alike to Homer and to the Egyptians and Hittites, are evidently the same people as those known to archaeology as Mycenaeans.

Neither archaeology nor foreign records tells us much about the internal organization of Mycenaean society, or indeed whether its members were authentic Greeks. For this information we must rely on the clay documents found in Mycenaean sites, first at Knossos and later in great quantities at Pylos in the southwestern corner of the Peloponnesus. These were deciphered in 1952 by a young English architect, Michael Ventris, who proved beyond doubt that they contain an archaic form of Greek. In one of the great tragedies of historical scholarship, Ventris was killed in 1956 in a road accident, but his epoch-making discovery had been made, and he left a rich legacy for others to develop.

The Mycenaean script, which is adapted from an earlier script current in Crete, whose reported decipherment has raised much controversy, is a syllabary, and its eighty-seven signs stand either for vowels or for consonants followed by vowels. Such a syllabary is far less efficient than an alphabet and contains many ambiguities owing to its lack of sufficient signs. This probably did not matter to its original users, who must have been officials who kept records only for certain purposes and were well acquainted with what the signs meant by convention. The documents are for the most part

TEXT CONTINUED ON PAGE 84

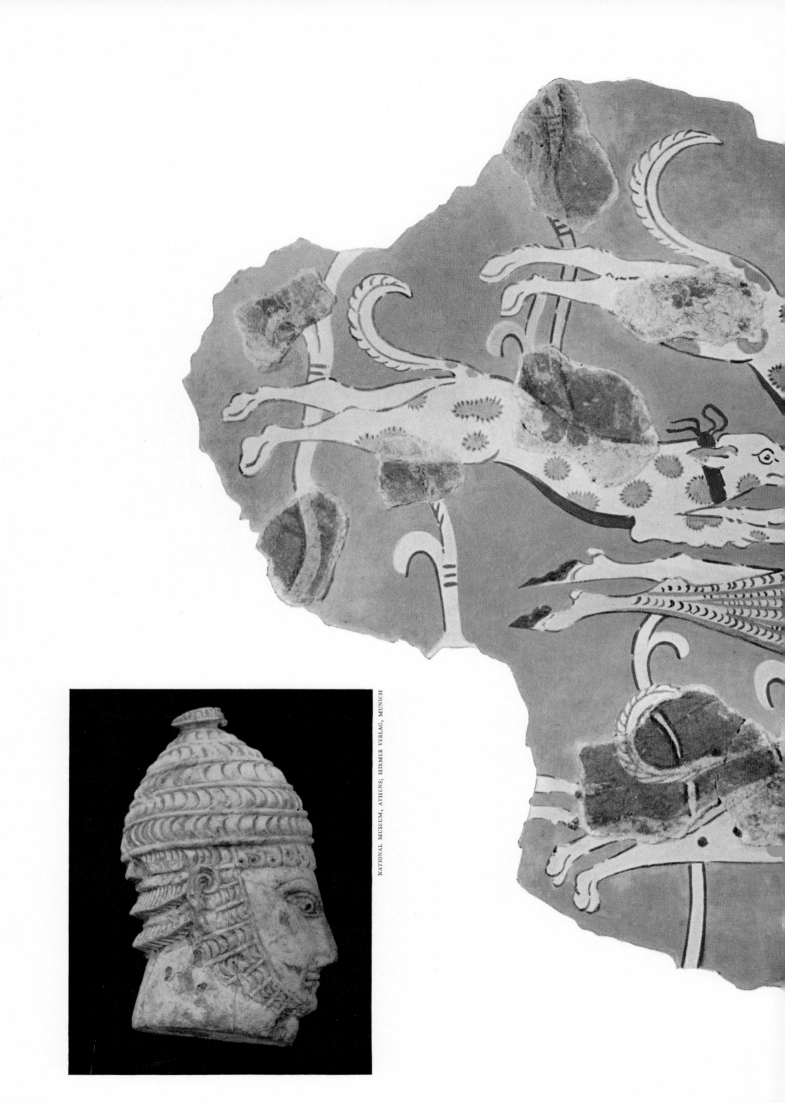

NATIONAL MUSEUM, ATHENS; HIRMER VERLAG, MUNICH

The Boar Hunt

Tracking the wild boar with hunting dogs was an exciting sport to the Mycenaean lord. The spectacle provided Homer with a simile for the Trojan attack on the Greeks:

> *"So two wild boars spring furious from their den,*
> *Roused with the cries of dogs and voice of men . . ."*

A painting of such a boar hunt adorned one wall of the palace of Tiryns, ten miles south of Mycenae. From the surviving fragments, which appear as dark spots in the picture, archaeologists made this reconstruction. Boars' teeth were prized for making helmets like that on the Mycenaean carved ivory figure (bottom left). Odysseus wore such a helmet in night operations against the Trojans. Homer reported, "A boar's white teeth grinn'd horrid o'er his head."

HARISSIADIS—NATIONAL MUSEUM, ATHENS

83

TEXT CONTINUED FROM PAGE 81

inventories of possessions, offerings to gods, documents on land tenure, military orders, and lists of men and women allotted to certain tasks. They contain not a trace of anything that can be called literature and have more than a touch of the précis in their manner. But their value is incalculable. They prove that the Mycenaeans were Greeks; that they had a highly organized system of government, were certainly quite as rich as Homer believed, worshiped some of the gods known to him, and had names very like those which he gives to Greeks and Trojans—including both Achilles and Hector, though neither of these has any claim to be Homer's original.

From these three sources we get, quite independently of Homer or other Greek source, a well-established notion of the Mycenaean world, of its wealth, its fine arts, its expanding and aggressive policies, and its ability to wage war. From it we may turn to the site of Troy and specifically to the level known as VIIa, a rebuilding of the city after the earthquake of circa 1280 B.C. This level keeps the old walls and gates, but has otherwise been refashioned for the needs of war. Empty spaces have been filled with houses; food supplies were kept in earthenware vessels dug into the floor; internal communications were improved by paved roads. About 1240 this city was destroyed by fire, and layers of ashes, calcined stones, burned bricks (to say nothing of corpses in the main

streets and under the walls) tell the same story. This was the Troy of which Homer knew, and its destruction was the work of invading Achaeans. It does not matter that it can have been no more than a fortress, covering some five acres. What matters is that it guarded the way into Asia, and the Achaeans captured and destroyed it. It was the last great event in their heroic legend. Story told that its capture cost the Achaeans dear, and that afterward disaster fell upon them. Within fifty years their great cities and fortresses of the mainland suffered the same fate as Troy, and the Mycenaean world came to an end. A few survivors escaped by sea to Ionia and brought with them the songs of their homeland and the memories of its heroic deeds.

It is of this heroic age that Homer tells, directly in the *Iliad* and less directly in the *Odyssey*. His information about it was extensive and surprising. He knew that Troy had been besieged and taken by an Achaean confederacy under the king of Mycenae, that among the Trojan allies were people who looked like Hittites, that Achaeans like Bellerophon had been active in an earlier generation in Asia Minor, that they did not hesitate to raid Egypt. He also knew more surprising details which meant nothing to his own age and can only be memories of the Mycenaean world. He consistently speaks of bronze weapons, and though he knows about iron, he does not mention that it was used for war. The helmets of his

King Nestor's Palace and Bathtub

PHOTOGRAPH BY ALISON FRANTZ

In Pylos, the traditional realm of the wise King Nestor, excavations have uncovered the remains of a sixty-room palace. The throne room in the foreground of the picture at left may be the hall where, in the Odyssey, *Nestor counseled Telemachus, Odysseus's son, in his search for his father. Upon his arrival at Pylos, the weary Telemachus was bathed by Polycaste, Nestor's beautiful daughter. A terracotta bathtub, decorated with spiral patterns and containing a broken kylix (right), found in the palace area lends reality to Homer's account of this ancient hospitality. King Nestor's palace was destroyed by fire around 1200 B.C.*

warriors have plumes and horns like those on the Warrior Vase from Mycenae (see page 80). His Ajax carries a shield "like a tower" (pages 74–75), which was normal in the fourteenth century but went out of use soon afterward. He speaks of such characteristic Mycenaean things as sword hilts riveted with silver or gold studs, of silver work inlaid with gold, of palaces with upper floors and rooms opening on vestibules and courtyards, of open precincts for the gods instead of temples. His shield of Achilles is made in a technique like that used in the inlaid dagger blades from Mycenae; he gives to Nestor a cup with images of doves on the rim, and such a cup, made of gold, has been found (see page 87). When he tells of the slaughter of men and animals at a great man's funeral, he is confirmed by a tomb at Dendra. He knows about the towers and gates of Troy and, more surprisingly, about the structure of its walls. Because of their unusual batter below the perpendicular ramparts, Patroclus is able to climb them up to the point where Apollo casts him down.

Homer knows of the gold of Mycenae, of the *temenos*, or special piece of land, allotted to princes and mentioned in Mycenaean documents, of thrones inlaid with ivory ornaments such as have been found in more than one place, of bronze greaves like those found in Cyprus and the Peloponnesus. He has heard of even remoter objects and situations. When Odysseus goes out on night operations, he wears a felt cap covered with boars' teeth (page 82); though such caps were common before 1300 B.C., they went out of use afterward. He gives an account of Egyptian Thebes which seems to come from the fourteenth century, when Amenhotep III decorated temples with floors and doors of gold and silver and built pylons which survive for Homer as a hundred gates. Homer's knowledge of the Mycenaean age is extensive, and through it he sets his story in a heroic past when men were wealthier and more powerful than in his own day.

At the same time many of Homer's details come from ages later than the Mycenaean. His dead are not buried but burned, a practice which seems to have started soon after the Trojan War. Though he knows about Thebes, he believes Egypt is so far away that even birds take a year to cross the sea from it. His warriors do not fight from chariots, like the Mycenaeans, but use them simply as a means of transport to places on the battlefield where they dismount and fight on foot. Instead of two horses his chariots usually have four. From his own time or near it come descriptions of the wealth of Apollo's shrine at Delphi, the Gorgon on the shield of Agamemnon, the wheeled tripods of Hephaestus, the advance of infantry in close line in battle, the structure of the brooch of Odysseus with its two pins fitting into sheaths, the part played by Phoenicians in the seafaring life of the *Odyssey*. Above all in his similes, which bear no relation to the

85

Mycenaean world, he draws from his own observation and touches on many subjects which lay outside his heroic theme but touched him intimately by their simple and varied appeal.

Why does Homer draw on the material of different centuries? How does he know anything about the Mycenaean world? The answers would be easy if we could believe that he inherited written texts of Mycenaean poems and that he drew upon them for material before bringing it up to date to suit his contemporary audience at points where it might be unintelligible. However, though the Mycenaeans used writing, there is no evidence that they used it for poetry, and, more important, it is clear that when the Mycenaean civilization perished, its system of writing perished with it. This is indeed an extraordinary, almost unparalleled phenomenon, and it can be explained only by the hypothesis that the scribes were a small class whose work the new conquerors did not understand and did not use. At any rate, on all the thousands of potsherds which originated between circa 1200 and 750 B.C., when the new Phoenician alphabet was introduced into Greece, there is not a single inscribed letter, and we are forced to conclude that Homer cannot have learned about the past from any written records. He may conceivably have seen some Mycenaean objects preserved as heirlooms, and he almost certainly knew the site of Troy (though not Ithaca), but even this would not account for his knowledge of the Mycenaean world. How did he find it?

As so often with Homer, the answer comes from looking at other oral poets who tell of the past. They do not learn from books; their knowledge of the past, which is often impressive, comes from oral tradition. Such a tradition may last for centuries, and this is what happened in Greece. We cannot doubt that heroic songs existed in the Mycenaean age, and it is even possible that the magnificent meter of the hexameter had already been invented, since Mycenaean Greek, as we can see from the tablets, falls easily into it. Bards passed on to their successors not only names and stories, metrical devices and tricks of narrative but something much more substantial and useful—a large number of formulaic phrases covering most needs of the heroic story and ready for use when the poet needed them. Such formulas were indispensable to oral composition and were fashioned with much care through many centuries until, by Homer's time, they met almost every want in his story. Oral poets operate less with single words than with phrases, and these phrases have been polished and perfected by generations until they have a true distinction of their own. Some of these formulas in Homer are extremely ancient, and he himself may not quite have known their original meaning, but they belonged to the tradition in which he learned his craft, and for that reason he used them. He could and no doubt did supplement them with new phrases of his own making, but these old formulas were his link with the past, and it is through them that he knew so much about an age which was at least five hundred years before his own. Whenever we come across something indubitably ancient in the *Iliad* or the *Odyssey*, we may be sure that it came to Homer through a long succession of bards whose art can be traced back to Mycenaean times.

Homer seems to have supplemented this traditional knowledge with a knowledge of the actual site of Troy. His story in the *Iliad* makes hardly any mistake in geography; and though many of the points may seem unimportant, like the course of the Scamander, or the distance from the city to the Achaean camp, or the plants and bushes on the plain, they

TEXT CONTINUED ON PAGE 93

"Mycenae, Rich in Gold"

Homer's admiration for the skill of Mycenaean goldsmiths is borne out by the treasure found in the tombs of the Grave Circle. The cup, which is reproduced a little larger than actual size on the facing page, is hammered from a single sheet of metal with handles bearing two golden birds. It is called "Nestor's Cup" because of its resemblance in miniature to the huge embossed goblet which the king of Pylos took with him to the Trojan battlefield.

> *"It was set with golden nails, the eared handles upon it were four,*
> *And on either side there were fashioned two doves of gold, feeding,*
> *And there were double bases beneath it.*
> *Another man with great effort could lift it full from the table,*
> *But Nestor, aged as he was, lifted it without strain."*　　　(Iliad, XI)

OVERLEAF: Two finely-wrought cups found at Vaphio depict the catching of wild bulls, probably for sacrifice to Poseidon, lord of the sea and protector of the Achaeans. Each cup is reproduced in actual size, with views of either side. On the left-hand page (top) a bull has been caught by the hind leg after succumbing to the lure of a captive cow (below). On the right-hand page (top) an angered bull flees after attacking his male and female captors (below). The Vaphio cups are in the National Museum in Athens.

HARISSIADIS–NATIONAL MUSEUM, ATHENS

Travelers to the World of Homer

A Visit to Homer's Birthplace

Anacharsis the younger, of Scythia, while voyaging along the Asiatic coast of the Aegean about 363 B.C., stopped at Chios.

"We dined one day at the house of one of the principal persons of the island, the conversation turned on the famous question of the country of Homer. Various cities and states aspired to the honor of having given birth to that celebrated man; but the claims of Chios are better founded than those of any other.

"Among their proofs of their validity, we were told that the descendants of Homer still remained in the island, and were known by the name of the Homeridae. At the same instant we saw two of them enter, habited with magnificent robes, and with golden crowns on their heads. They did not rehearse the eulogium of the poet, but offered to him a more precious incense. After an invocation to Jupiter, they sang alternately several select extracts from the *Iliad*, and performed their parts with such judgment and propriety, that we discovered new beauties in the passages that had before excited our admiration."

Alexander at Troy

Alexander the Great was so devoted to Homer that he always slept with a copy of the Iliad *(along with a dagger) under his pillow. Plutarch describes his visit to Ilium in the fourth century* B.C.

"Then, going up to Ilium, he sacrificed to Athena and poured libations to the heroes. Furthermore, the gravestone of Achilles he anointed with oil, ran a race by it with his companions, naked, as is the custom, and then crowned it with garlands, pronouncing the hero happy in having, while he lived, a faithful friend, and after death, a great herald of his fame. As he was going about and viewing the sights of the city, someone asked him if he wished to see the lyre of Paris. 'For that lyre,' said Alexander, 'I care very little; but I would gladly see that of Achilles, to which he used to sing the glorious deeds of brave men.'"

From Lady Mary Wortley Montague

In 1716 Lady Mary Wortley Montague accompanied her husband in his embassy to Turkey. To her friend Alexander Pope, who translated Homer into English, she wrote from Adrianople:

"I read over your Homer here with an infinite pleasure, and find several little passages explained, that I did not before entirely comprehend the beauty of; many of the customs, and much of the dress then in fashion, being yet retained. . . . the princesses and great ladies pass their time at their looms, embroidering veils and robes, surrounded by their maids, which are always very numerous, in the same manner as we find Andromache and Helen described. The description of the belt of Menelaus exactly resembles those that are now worn by the great

men, fastened before with broad golden clasps, and embroidered round with rich work. The snowy veil that Helen throws over her face, is still fashionable; and I never see (as I do very often) half a dozen of old pashas with their reverend beards, sitting basking in the sun, but I recollect good King Priam and his counsellors."

Byron to Homer's Defense

Lord Byron became convinced by his own journeys through Greece and Troy, that Homer's geography was authentic. There were factions in England who doubted it strongly, however, and Byron disagreed vehemently with Jacob Bryant who published in 1796 "A Dissertation concerning the war of Troy, and the expedition of the Grecians, as described by Homer; shewing, that no such expedition was ever undertaken, and that no such city of Phrygia existed."

In "Don Juan," Byron wrote:

"I've stood upon Achilles' tomb,
And heard Troy doubted;
Time will doubt of Rome."

Earlier in the poem Byron described the shores of Ilium.

"There, on the green and village-cotted hill, is
(Flanked by the Hellespont, and by the sea)
Entombed the bravest of the brave, Achilles;
They say so—(Bryant says the contrary):
And further downward, tall and towering still, is
The tumulus—of whom? Heaven knows! 't may be
Patroclus, Ajax, or Protesilaus—
All heroes, who if living still would slay us."

Keats on Chapman's Translation

The Pope version of Homer did not please John Keats, who considered it inferior to his own abilities. In the autumn of 1816, Charles Cowden Clarke invited Keats to look at a beautiful folio edition of Chapman's translation of Homer. Clarke and Keats delved into it until the early morning. The following day Clarke found an envelope placed on his desk in Keats's handwriting, with this enclosure:

"On first looking into Chapman's Homer"

"Much Have I travell'd in the Realms of Gold,
And many goodly states, and kingdoms seen;
Round many Western islands have I been
Which bards in fealty to Apollo hold.
Oft of one wide expanse had I been told
Which deep-brow'd Homer ruled as his Demesne;
Yet could I never judge what Men could mean,
Till I heard Chapman speak out loud and bold.

Then felt I like some watcher of the Skies
When a new Planet swims into his ken;
Or like stout Cortez, when with wond'ring eyes
He star'd at the Pacific, and all his Men
Look'd at each other with a wild surmise
Silent upon a Peak in Darien."

This death mask was found by Schliemann on a skeleton in one of the royal tombs at Mycenae. Always quick with a romantic designation, Schliemann called it the Mask of Agamemnon, and so it has been known ever since. It does have the appearance of an individual portrait and a majesty of countenance sufficient to command the obedience of Homeric warriors.

NAL MUSEUM, ATHENS; HIRMER VERLAG, MUNICH

TEXT CONTINUED FROM PAGE 86

all indicate that he knew more about the battlefield than even his formulas can have given him. Indeed, even today, when we stand on the ruins of Troy and look over the plain, we feel that we can see why his masterpiece fits so well into the landscape. The Troy he saw was certainly in ruins, but he knew that it had been a great city, and he took advantage of his local knowledge to create such scenes as those of Andromache on the tower seeing the dead body of her husband dragged behind the chariot of Achilles or Priam going out at night across the plain to ransom the body of his dead son from the terrible man who has killed him. Among these ruins, which were old even in his time, Homer created again an ancient tale and gave to it a strength which it surely never had before.

Homer is not a historian, and he lived long before scientific history was invented. His re-creation of the past in poetry is not historical because it combines competing elements which come from some six centuries. No doubt, too, he made his own improvements on legends, and we have no right to presume that all he says is true. What he tells is what he himself believed because the Muse had told it to him. By the Muse he means the divine power of creative song which he knew in himself and rightly regarded as the daughter of Memory, because it was indeed a people's memory that had preserved so much for him. We do not know how he performed his songs. He himself makes bards sing to kings at their courts, and perhaps this is what he himself did, though it would not prevent him from singing also at religious festivals and public gatherings. Nor do we know how his poems were written down. It is most unlikely that his pupils memorized them and passed them by word of mouth to later generations, since for this there is no parallel in oral performance; indeed, it is alien to the methods of such composition. The easiest explanation is that since he himself was alive when the wonderful art of writing returned to the Greeks in the form of the Phoenician alphabet, he dictated his poems to someone who knew it and the written texts were guarded by professional bards who recited them to later generations. Yet he remains an oral poet who uses all the devices of this special craft and draws his art from a long tradition. His aim was more to delight than to instruct, but he believed that men delighted to hear of the glorious doings of men and that such doings, and the sufferings which they bring, find a reward and a consolation in song. To this task he gave his incomparable gifts. He learned the ancient formulas and used them as if they were fresh as the morning for his vision of the heroic generations who once belonged to his race and whose memory was treasured through all the changes and catastrophes of the intervening years.

Sir Maurice Bowra, a leading scholar of the ancient Greek world, is warden of Wadham College, Oxford. His books include Problems in Greek Poetry *and* Heroic Poetry. *His latest work,* The Greek Experience, *evaluates the Greek spirit through its philosophy, from the time of Homer to the fall of Athens in the year 404* B.C.

She could be Helen

But all we know is that she adorned a wall of the palace of Tiryns in the thirteenth century B.C. *Starting with fragments, which appear as darker areas, archaeologists used other paintings as a guide to reconstruct the figure of a stately, curly-haired woman. She wears the embroidered, open-bodiced dress that Mycenaean women adopted from Crete.*

THE MYCENAEAN WORLD C. 1400 B.C.

Scale

0   50   100   150 Miles

ON THE NEXT THREE SPREADS: SCENES OF HOMER'S EPICS

The Site of the Trojan War

"I have an unshakable faith in Homer," declared Heinrich Schliemann when he set out to discover the site of ancient Troy. Following Homer's clue that the Achaeans often made seven or eight journeys a day from the seashore to the besieged city, he fixed upon the hill of Hissarlik at the southeastern shore of the Dardanelles. There, in 1873, he uncovered a city of nine layers, of which he took the second oldest to be the city of Priam. It remained for the University of Cincinnati expedition, digging in the 1930's under the direction of Carl W. Blegen, to establish that a higher level, labeled Troy VIIa, was in fact the Homeric citadel. Shattered houses, crushed bodies, and a Mycenaean arrowhead gave evidence of the sudden destruction which came to it about 1240 B.C.

In the picture on the opposite page, taken in 1902, a Turk stands on ancient stones uncovered by the early excavations. Behind him stretches the plain where Priam went forth to beg the body of his son Hector from the wrathful Achilles. The Attic vase above of circa 490 B.C. shows Hector's body beneath Achilles' bedstead, with the aged king making his plea:

> *"For him through hostile camps I bent my way,*
> *For him thus prostrate at thy feet I lay;*
> *Think of thy father, and this face behold!*
> *See him in me, as helpless and as old!"*

> (Iliad, *XXIV*)

Lands of the Odyssey

The mountainous island whose indented coastline appears in the foreground on the opposite page is usually identified as Odysseus's homeland. Mycenaean potsherds have been found on the island, as well as a terra-cotta fragment of an ex-voto bearing a prayer to Odysseus—evidence that the name was held to be divine there. But the identification is uncertain, as is almost all the geography in the Odyssey.

Whether or not there was ever a historical Odysseus, the Odyssey *is primarily a work of fiction. Its hero is guided at every step by Athena and is ever in conflict with supernatural beings, as in the scene above from a fifth-century B.C. vase. Here one of the Sirens swoops down on Odysseus, who has tied himself to the ship's mast in order to resist the Sirens' fatal song, while his sailors have plugged their ears with wax to escape the same enchantment.*

Though the Odyssey *is not subject, as the* Iliad *is, to the confirmation of archaeology, it nevertheless fits into the scholars' unfolding picture of the Mycenaean world. In the years before the Trojan War, Mycenae looked eastward to the Aegean islands and the coast of Asia Minor. But after the war, and especially after the Dorian invasions a century later, it looked westward to Sicily, Italy, and the new Greek colonies of the central Mediterranean. The* Odyssey *reflects this new orientation of the Greek world.*

The Home of the Gods

The gods of Homer are the same willful, quarrelsome, all too "human" gods who composed the pantheon of classical Greece. The poet speaks of other divinities, too—river-gods and wood nymphs from an earlier nature worship—but these are clearly lesser beings, outside the Olympian circle. The decipherment of Linear B script gave scholars their first proof that Homer's names for the gods were those used by the Mycenaeans. On tablets they have found the names of Zeus, Athena, Hermes, Hera, Poseidon, Artemis, and Dionysus—enough to establish the presumption that the entire pantheon was formed in Mycenaean times.

Homer's anthropomorphic gods and goddesses dwelt in the far north of Greece, "where old Olympus shrouds his hundred heads in heaven, and props the clouds." To the eye of the modern camera, Mount Olympus is a grim and jagged pinnacle streaked with snow and cloaked in mist, but the gods dwelt there in perpetual springtime. The classic vase below, from the sixth century B.C., shows them in assembly. Zeus, crowned and bearded, holding his thunderbolts in his left hand, receives his ceremonial nectar from the cupbearer, Ganymede. Behind the boy are Hestia, goddess of the hearth, holding a vine branch and flower; Aphrodite, holding a dove; and Ares the war-god, bearing his Corinthian helmet and lance. Behind Zeus are Athena, goddess of wisdom; Hermes, the winged-sandaled messenger; and Hebe, the daughter of Zeus and goddess of youth.

On Stage: DAVID HURST

Of *Brouhaha,* an off-Broadway play that ran for its life for two nights, and lost, critic Walter Kerr wrote: "Let us not speak of [it]. Ever. Let us speak of David Hurst. After a first act that seems no longer than 'Hawaii,' Mr. Hurst arrives upon the scene to aid the dead and the dying, some of whom are on the stage and some of whom are in the audience. . . . It is perfectly clear that we have an actor in our midst."

"I was embarrassed to show up the next evening," said Hurst, a thirty-four-year-old character actor who conceivably could summon a bashful blush to the roots of his brindled mane if a role called for it. Off stage he keeps to a muted ruddiness, with brows and mustache the frazzled gold of costume braid that has weathered more than a few long runs (an experience Hurst has yet to have in this country).

"David is the most discovered actor in America," a friend has observed. "Every time he is seen in another part, and he has been seen, emphatically, in several since he came over from London, he is 'discovered' all over again." Hurst's first Broadway role was a seven-minute—and, as it turned out, a show-stopping seven-minute—bit as an elaborately Gallic police inspector in Noël Coward's *Look After Lulu,* a play that set no attendance records. For this Hurst won the 1959 Clarence Derwent Award for the best performance by a non-featured actor. He was so non-featured that he was not even listed in the program notes.

David Hurst has since played in four off-Broadway productions: the brother in Chekhov's *Three Sisters;* an epicurean Soviet ambassador in the aforementioned *Brouhaha;* an ant who is a scientist in *Under the Sycamore Tree;* and in a program of two short plays by Ionesco, a surrealist suburban type in *The Bald Soprano* and Jack's father in *Jack.* At the Margo Jones Theater in Dallas he played a rascally seventy-year-old Cockney in *Physician for Fools,* and on the road he played Britannicus to Franchot Tone's and Susan Strasberg's *Caesar and Cleopatra.* His television roles have been equally varied: the war-mongering poet in *Tiger at the Gates;* one of a pair of twin Hungarian interrogators with beards in *The Emperor's Clothes;* a bumptious English lawyer in *A Tale of Two Cities;* and a companion of Mark Twain in *Roughing It.* His current assignment—*on* Broadway, for once—is the role of Merlyn in *Camelot.*

Hurst's success with such a chameleon array of accents, ages, and character traits is rooted in his definition of acting. "To be an honest actor," he says, "you have to subjugate the need to be 'recognized' to the needs of the role. Many actors aren't willing to neutralize their own voice and personality to a part. It runs counter to the star system." For a part, Hurst will—and can—grow a background as readily as a beard; with rubbery ease he can seemingly lose or recover an *embonpoint,* be halt or nimble as occasion demands.

A character actor may be defined as an actor of extraordinary, one might say aurora borealis, range. "There are a handful in every generation," writer George Sherman said recently, "and I think David will belong to that handful. In London he acted in some twenty movies and many plays—his last was the lead, as Ustinov's replacement, in *Romanoff and Juliet.* But he left London because he felt he was being typed. He sounds English to us, but he was born in Berlin and usually played Continental types. Here, casting procedures being what they are, it might help him if he fit into some kind of pigeon hole. Look at Alex Guinness, a great character actor—if you saw him on the street, would you know how to cast him?"

Walking down a street, wearing a British felt cap and momentarily resembling nothing so much as an unattenuated Rowland Emett character who might at any moment pull aboard an attenuated Emett trolley and head someplace for kippers, Hurst added his own comment: "America is so vast that if a casting agent wants a man with a carbuncle under his right ear, he can find one—immediately."

Hurst's father had been general secretary of the Berlin Theater Association in pre-Hitler Germany, as well as a critic and journalist; his mother was a fashion-magazine editor. In 1939 the boy was sent to Ireland, where he completed four years of art school and where, at seventeen, he played his first part in a Belfast production of *Watch on the Rhine.* The director's advice "not to fidget" was the extent of his training as an actor. When he was eighteen he joined the Royal Irish Fusiliers, but toward the end of the war he was assigned to an army entertainment unit.

He is married to a New York girl whom he met in London while she was covering openings as a free-lance Broadway scout. They have two very young daughters to whom Hurst reads, according to his wife, "as no one else can—with accents, growls, and gestures."

Hurst's intensity provides the clue to his transformation into so many selves. "An actor draws on his warehouse of experiences, suffering, love," he says, "but acting is not therapy. On stage the actor must project *another* person, someone whose wheeze or limp or way of buttoning his coat or closing his mind—whatever—has been absorbed by studying people, by reading, by knowing the books and paintings and plays of a given place and era. Acting is thinking until you get a headache."

"He also has an idea of what he is doing," Brooks Atkinson once observed, and on another occasion saluted him for "having a clear point of view . . . at the center of a general muddle." It is the kind of lucidity that promises, someday, incandescence.   MARYBETH WESTON

Photograph by EUGENE COOK

GOTTSCHO—SCHLEISNER

*For all their gaudy splendor,
modern vacation hotels fail to match
the grandeur of the old resorts*

THE PEOPLE'S PALACES

By MARSHALL B. DAVIDSON

SAM FALK

Modern resorts come in two styles: the bold and the shrinking. The Fontainebleau, pronounced by many of its guests "Fountain Blue" (left), is a flamboyant descendant of the hotels built in the Gilded Age (see following pages). Its architect, Morris Lapidus, is the leading designer of this style. Caneel Bay Plantation (below) is so scattered and so camouflaged with palm trees that it almost disappears in the landscape of St. John, Virgin Islands. Built with Rockefeller money, it is typical of many of the new Caribbean resorts.

Among the nomadic peoples of the world, none has raised such a variety of interesting and curious monuments to mark its seasonal treks as the Americans. From the gingerbread fairylands of Saratoga Springs to the marble tents of Las Vegas, resort hotels stand as monuments to the democratic longing for a life of princely luxury. As architecture, these pleasure domes have ever tended towards a parody of the constructions we live in at home, ranging from masterpieces to absurdities.

The scene changes swiftly. In Miami Beach, so recently reclaimed from the swamps, the "old" hotels with several seasons' hard use are constantly remodeled to meet the challenge of this year's newly built attraction. Like so many Mad Hatters, the seasonal visitors turn restlessly from the soiled tea-cup to a fresh one. And along the expanding perimeter of the vacation belt, especially in the southern arc, architectural innovations sprout with the lush profusion of tropical flora. One can hide out, very roughly speaking, in carefully contrived informal surroundings, or one can rent by the day, week, or month, a section of Paradise, so advertised, that cost twenty million dollars to provide and that tries to look like the money. In the latest creations one can even get away from the soft, southern breezes by turning on the air conditioner, trading winds as it were. Yet, as the photographs on the following pages recall, none of these latter-day palaces quite achieve the grandeur of the older resorts.

It was the magic touch of the railroads as they fingered their way through the land that brought most of the first great resorts to life. Some of these early landmarks, bearing traces of the Pullman-car eclecticism of their heyday, still survive in the web of thruways and air lanes of the present. When the Hotel del Coronado was opened in 1888 near San Diego, a stop on the Santa Fe, its architecture was described as of "a mixed character, partaking largely of the Queen Anne style, and having also much that is characteristic of the Elizabethan era" along with "many of the excellences of other schools, both ancient and modern." At the time, in any case, it was the largest of the West Coast resort hotels, and to its variegated splendors came four presidents of the United States, the king of Hawaii, and assorted merchant princes of the highest rank.

That same year, 1888, Henry Morrison Flagler opened "the world's finest hotel" the Ponce de Leon, at Saint Augustine in distant Florida. To facilitate the construction of this pile, designed by Carrère and Hastings "in the style of the Spanish Renaissance," and to provide access for its guests, Flagler purchased and rehabilitated a parcel of small railroads. Over a million dollars after the project was started, a great omnibus drawn by six white horses brought the first customers from the railroad station; as the gates of the palace rose, cannons boomed, orchestras played "The Star-Spangled Banner," and Floridians rejoiced. With its elaborately sculptured woodwork, its stair walls of solid polished marble, its stained-glass windows, and its electric lights, all enclosed by three-foot-thick walls of poured concrete, it set, they said, a new standard in American architecture.

Flagler continued to promote Florida as a winter playground for the rich, building such other resplendent hostelries as The Breakers and the Royal Poinciana at Palm Beach. The first guests to reach the Poinciana over the new Flagler Bridge in 1896 comprised a select private trainful of seventeen socialites, including four Vanderbilts, although the hotel was the largest wooden structure in history and was built to accommodate 1750 people.

Cornelius Vanderbilt, another sound-thinking railroad man, had opened the Grand Hotel on Mackinac Island in northern Michigan nine years before. If a sweeping veranda is the most consistently recurrent feature of our "classical" resort architecture, the Grand, with its 885-foot long colonnaded porch is the archetype of all such retreats. The railroads never actually reached the island, and automobiles are banned. Here one can step back, after a fashion, into the Victorian past; and among Midwesterners it is still a fashionable step to take.

You can drive a car to the Mountain House on Lake Mohonk, high in the Shawangunk Mountains not far from New York City, but not on Sunday; and you can't get a drink there any day of the week. As its first announcements clearly stated, this was a retreat in a stricter sense of the word, built as a "Temperance House . . . for the refined and moral classes, where they can enjoy the splendid scenery of the lake without molestation from the faster and rougher elements of society." And as early editions of *Baedeker's United States* warned, here were held semiannual conferences to "discuss International Arbitration and the means of improving the condition of the American Indian. . . . Moreover, 'visitors are not expected to arrive or depart on the Sabbath.'"

Many such great timber resorts sprang up at picturesque spots everywhere in the nation during the last quarter of the nineteenth century in direct response to a spirit of romanticism and a sense of moral purpose. As civilization plundered its way across the continent, a growing number of Americans turned to what was left of nature to quiet their spirits and refresh their souls. For nature, as Emerson counseled his countrymen, was "the circumstance which dwarfs every other circumstance, and judges like a god all men that come to her."

Even organized religion played its part in adding variety to American resorts. Before giving up forever any attempt to chart the complexities of the American scene, Baedeker's guide referred to Ocean Grove, established in 1870 by the Methodist Episcopal Church on the New Jersey coast, as an "extraordinary settlement, possible only in America, in which many thousands of persons, young and old, voluntarily elect to spend their summer vacations under a religious autocracy, which is severe both in its positive and negative regulations." No drinking, no tobacco, no theater, and, on Sundays, no bathing, riding, or driving; a place, Baedeker concluded, "curious enough to repay a short visit"—as it still is.

HILTON INTERNATIONAL

Left: At Las Brisas in Acapulco, now owned by Hilton International, almost every cottage has a private swimming pool. Opposite: The veranda of the Grand Union Hotel at Saratoga Springs was a favorite parade ground of Society in the 1890's.

OLD SPAIN IN FLORIDA

The Ponce de Leon in Saint Augustine was the first of the hotels commissioned by Henry Morrison Flagler to lure vacationers to Florida via the Flagler railroad. The two young architects John Merven Carrère and Thomas Hastings, who subsequently built New York City's Public Library, responded to their commission with an exuberence they never attempted in their later creations. With two belfried towers

THE DINING ROOM

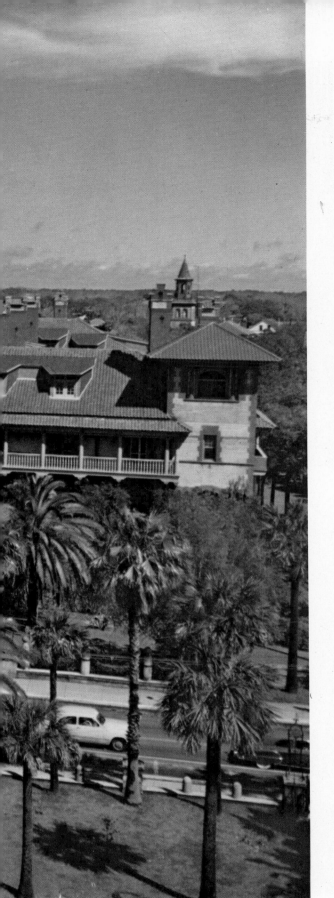

PHOTOGRAPHS HANNAU COLOR PRODUCTIONS

rising above an immense inner court, solid concrete walls faced with coquina (a local shell rock), and an uninhibited variety of interior decoration, they transformed the spirit of old Spain into a gay reverie of America's Age of Elegance. Most of the rich and varied ornament was conceived by Bernard Maybeck, an associate whose fertile imagination practically forced the architects to take unexpected liberties with their theme.

THE GRAND HOTEL *on Mackinac Island, Michigan*

THE BREAKERS *in Palm Beach*

CULVER PICTURES INC.

THE PROUD GIANTS

During the last decades of the nineteenth century, America broke out in a luxuriant growth of holiday retreats. North, East, South, and West—wherever the railroads reached and a bit beyond—public palaces sprang up to receive and entertain the well-heeled vacationer. All of the establishments shown on these pages, except for the Grand Union at Saratoga Springs (page 105), are still going strong. Some, like the Mount Washington and the Coronado, have become primarily convention hotels, but the others still cater to a private, if less socially exclusive, clientele.

THE MOUNT WASHINGTON *at Bretton Woods, N. H.*

THE HOTEL DEL CORONADO *near San Diego*

EWING GALLOWAY

CULVER PICTURES INC.

OVERLEAF: The Mountain House, still an active resort on Lake Mohonk in New York's Shawangunk Mountains, offered desirable guests in the 1890's "the comforts of a good home, at reasonable rates" (in season, singles from $18 to $30 a week, doubles from $36 to $50). Although dogs and liquor were banned, many distinguished New York families registered there for a summer holiday. To see and to be seen from a veranda was part of the vacation experience. The Mountain House boasted more than 400 feet of broad piazzas for public use, and most lodgings had private balconies.

BROWN BROTHERS; OVERLEAF, HANNAU COLOR PRODUCTIONS

A wealth of good timber was squandered on the building of American resorts. The remote extremes are represented by the jigsaw lacework of the Spray View House in Ocean Grove, New Jersey (above), where devout fanatics came to enjoy "God's Square Mile of Health & Happiness," and by the monumental rustic construction of the Glacier Na-tional Park Hotel in Montana (below). The Glacier Park opened its doors early in the century to guests who arrived in jinrikishas and who were ushered into a "forested" lobby lined by great natural columns. Japanese lanterns, bearskins, Navaho rugs, and mounted animal skulls contributed other decorative accents to a life of luxury in the Wild West.

THE CRITIC'S VIEW

THEATER

The Roaring Presence of Brendan Behan

". . . this period of our early manhood, perhaps the most impressionable years of one's life, was an age of revolution. . . . We felt ourselves to be the second generation in this exciting movement of men and ideas. . . . After the 1914 war, and still more after Hitler's war, the young who are not conservatives, fascists, or communists are almost certainly defeatist; they have grown up under the shadow of defeat in the past and the menace of defeat in the future. It is natural, inevitable that they should suffer from the sterility of being angry young men."

Thus Leonard Woolf, in *Sowing*, the first volume of his memoirs, contrasts Lytton Strachey, Clive Bell, John Maynard Keynes, and the other elegant intellectuals of Cambridge just at the turn of the century with the young influential spirits he sees around him today. And thus, from some distance in time and climate, I approach the roaring presence of Brendan Behan. I doubt that Behan would have found himself suitably employed passing tea and advanced sentiments in a Trinity College study, and I feel certain that Woolf's circle would have found little to commend in Behan's *Hostage*, which blasted Broadway back into life last September. And yet of all the writers who have come up since World War II Behan has the best right, I think, to identify himself with Woolf's words.

Behan is in rebellion against establishment and propriety; his heroes are tough and disreputable, his speech is rude, and his ability to seize and shake the imagination of his time is prodigious. It is convenient then, almost to the point of being inevitable, that he should be thought of in company with such marauding talents of the day as Beckett, Gênet, and John Osborne. But the association is more evident than it is comfortable. These others, whatever their differences of manner and attainment, have in common a vision of society in decay: their scenes smell of bad teeth and septic flesh, and the condition they diagnose does not seem to be reversible. Furthermore, diagnosis is the function they perform. They do not rebel from within a community; they have removed themselves in order to draw up a report, a forecast, if necessary an epitaph. The loneliness such men endure in their work is in itself a heroic renunciation.

There is none of that in Behan. He insults you with his arm around your shoulder and invites you to join in a song dedicated to your own asininity. He himself is always felt to be in the thick of his plays, and he throws abuse and ridicule on authority and respectability as though blasphemy were his native tongue. In a real sense it is—unlike the others, Behan was born and raised in revolution. Rebellion is not associated in his mind with lonely withdrawal and frustrated rage; it is the way you join your pals and get the job done. It is easy today to laugh at the Irish Nationalists —and Behan, who is no professional Irishman for all his blarney, is a leader in the laughter; but it should be remembered that they carried out the only successful war of independence which the West has known in our century. Behan recently remarked to a New York reporter, "The first duty of a writer is to let his country down. He knows his own people the best. He has a special responsibility to let them down." Behan doesn't say this sort of thing just to be outrageous; it is an expression of his real patriotism. He is loyal to the subversive principle in human affairs and has gone to jail in its behalf.

The difference between Behan and his contemporaries is not a matter of excellence. Certainly, on the basis of what he has done so far, I would not give him place as an artist over the others. I cannot help feeling that his cocksnookery is more valid than the clammy, irresolute whining that pervades Osborne's work; yet Beckett's man alone among the lunar stones, and the grinning obscenities of Gênet's paradoxes, may be our truer monuments.

But views of the future are not only prophetic; they are aspects of our present temper and can have an effect on our course. In the midst of death we are still alive, and Behan's subversion explains why his pull on the audience is close to irresistible. Irreverence has almost disappeared from our common speech and we miss the salt of it. When the curtain of *The Hostage* went up last fall on a spectacle of whores, odd boys, and assorted ruffians dancing a jig with the innocent pleasure of children let out of school, a rush of blood seemed to sweep through the stagnant arteries of Broadway. We were back again at the old business of being the vulgar, raucous, incorrigible children of God.

The story, as must be known by now, concerns a young English soldier, seized as hostage for an Irish lad who has had the bad judgment to shoot a policeman and who is about to hang for it. The Cockney boy is brought to an old I.R.A. hide-out, now converted from lack of patriotic funds to a bawdy house, and there takes part in the general larking about while waiting final word on the fate of his opposite number. The English hostage dies in a bitterly pointless accident. But the plot is only a trampoline from which Behan can launch gymnastic sallies against crowned heads and commissars, churchmen, patrioteers, and dreamers. The play is staged by Joan Littlewood, director of the Theatre Workshop in London, in a style of danced reality, a choreography of personality at full tilt, that makes much of our local work look solemn and lumpy.

It could be that Behan is too much aware that his mission is to liven things up a bit. He reminds you at times of the guest who takes to throwing the cold cuts about on the misapplied theory that a touch of wit will save the party. Pretty much anything goes at *The Hostage*, and what rescues it is the speed with which the author recovers from his lapses. Perhaps there is a theory here— that Behan is a phenomenon of nature and not to be distilled through art. If so, it is arrogance—a peculiar virus for a man of Behan's comic sense to pick up.

The play recalls a good many sources: it is part music-hall turn, part gaslight melodrama; it inherits an attitude from O'Casey and derives incidents from Behan's own life and from the morning papers (lines change a bit as the weeks pass). It is as slapdash as a club amateur night, with the action stopping any time someone wants to belt out a song, the characters making broad-winked asides to the audience, and the dead hero hopping up at the end so that everyone can go home happy. Behan is quite willing to coax a laugh out of someone's inability to get to the toilet, and he doesn't hesitate to milk the sentiment of two homeless orphans falling sweetly into love (and, since it is Behan writing, also into bed). He sees nothing odd about putting a bawdy song into the mouth of a convent girl from the country. *The Hostage* does not subscribe to the laws of classic unity.

And yet the point and drive of the thing belie its squatter carpentry. Behan doesn't set his stage in a brothel to catch onto a stylish cliché, nor does he have a mad Anglo-Irishman skirling bagpipes through the proceedings from wistful memories of *You Can't Take It With You*. He doesn't break into his action with implausible arias, or otherwise shatter the stage illusion, by inadvertence. He does these things because the remnants of the I.R.A. are the sons of heroes sunk into seediness, crazy with the wail of old glories and falling out of the frame of reality like fragments from a cracked mirror. And by implication that is the status of fanatic nationalism everywhere—it is a passion that has outrun its time.

Pat, the caretaker of the rooming house and former comrade-in-arms of Monsewer, the daft piper, is closest to being Behan's own voice in the play. Meg, his old girl, says to him:

"You're always singing about them ould times, and the five glorious years, and still you sneer and jeer at the boys nowadays. What's the difference?"

And he answers:

"The H-Bomb. I'm nervous of it. It's such a big bomb it's after making me scared of little bombs. The I.R.A. is out of date and so is the R.A.F. So is the Swiss Guard and the Foreign Legion, the Red Army, the United States Marines, the Free State Army."

Behan throws in rousing ballads about Michael Collins and Easter Week; but he also sings "Don't muck about with the moon" and "There's no place on earth like the world," and those are the songs you remember. Behan the boy terrorist, captured in Liverpool at the age of sixteen with a suitcase full of dynamite, has changed the focus of his outlawry. He is being subversive on the side of sweet reason and a little more tolerance, please, before we blow ourselves off the map.

The particular quality of Behan's tolerance is the most attractive thing about him and the mortar that holds his jackstraw constructions together. It has nothing to do with innocence or indifference; he possesses an encyclopedic knowledge of mischief and depravity and, though unconcerned by copybook morality, is implacable in the face of real wickedness. The tolerance that sustains his writing and gives it a health uncommon in our day stems from a rueful confidence in man's ability to be decent in a modest sort of way. I attribute it to the teaching of his early prison years.

As Behan points out in the autobiographic *Borstal Boy*, England can maintain its boast of having no prisons for political prisoners by the expedient of throwing such politicals as it wishes to punish into the common pool of felons. Thus, when he was put away over the matter of the suitcase, Behan was sent to a Borstal Institution, where he found himself in the company of a desperate sample of Britain's youth. Thieves predominated, but there was also a substantial representation of armed robbers, pimps, murderers, and rapists. Behan was no lamb among the wolves—he had been reared in the streets of Dublin and the ranks of an illegal army—but he was a clean and honest boy who went to confession regularly (until the English put a stop to that). However, he was also obsessively gregarious—if pimps and murderers were the only society available, then pimps and murderers must be his friends. He moved in with his fists and his songs and found that where he assumed good faith he usually found it.

Behan was probably lucky to be thrown in with criminal society at this youngest level; ten years later he might not have found his way so easily behind the masks. But having once seen men in terms of what can be expected of them if you don't ask too much, he has never lost his bias of modest optimism. Years later in *The Quare Fellow*, that coldeyed attack on capital punishment, Behan constructs horror and pity out of small vignettes of courtesy, tact, humor, slyness, and above all tolerance. And so in *The Hostage* he mixes wit and foolishness, pomposity and humor, selfishness and compassion, until you can't tell the saints from the sinners and are reduced to blessing them all. Behan, who never misses a chance to catch the church under the ribs, calls himself a Christian. It is this faith in the not excessive decency of unremarkable men that he means.

—ROBERT HATCH

MOVIES

The Hindu Trilogy

With *The World of Apu,* Satyajit Ray brings his Hindu trilogy to an impressive end. The end, however, is as inconclusive as life itself, and one feels that the brilliant director-writer-producer could continue his saga indefinitely. In the first of the three lyrical, pensive, and uncompromisingly realistic films, *Pather Panchali,* we meet Apu as a village child in the household of impoverished Brahmins. His gentle father is scholarly, his oppressed mother toils ceaselessly and joylessly to keep her family one step from death by starvation; there is an aunt, so old and gaunt and twisted that for some reels it is hard to know whether we are looking at a man or a woman. We observe Apu and his older sister engaged in the universal antics and solemn contemplations of childhood: the petty thefts of fruit and trinkets, the running through fields in the rain, the wondering study of trains hooting their high dirge as they race toward unimaginable cities. The ancient aunt dies, and so, far more tragically, does Apu's sister. The end of the film shows the boy and his parents in a decrepit cart piled with their pathetic lares and penates going along a country road on their way to Benares. Into their abandoned house, a cobra insinuates its evil way.

In *Aparajito,* Apu as a young man experiences the glamour and the vicissitudes of city life and student life: he works at exhausting jobs; he bathes, exhilarated, in the Ganges. His father falls ill and dies. Apu wins a scholarship to the university in Calcutta, and he is there when his mother also dies, leaving him now completely alone. Although this picture was visually as remarkable as the first, I found it much less satisfactory. There were innumerable arresting vignettes of the confused urban life, the tortuous old alleys thronged with muti-

lated beggars and skinny children whose faces were all big dark eyes, the filthy shops and markets and the foul tenements teeming with wretched, hopeless life. Memorable and disturbing as all this was, the sequel to *Pather Panchali* lacked the impact of the first.

Apu is waking up in his lower-depths room at the beginning of *The World of Apu.* Rain pours upon him through the window curtained with a torn rag. When he finally accomplishes the transition from sleep to consciousness, he removes his shirt from beneath the mattress where it has been protected from the rain, and he shaves, using as a bowl what appears to be a sardine tin. Apu is now a man; otherwise, his estate is the same as ever, and he is still alone. But presently, exquisite beauty enters his life, and for a while he is elevated from suffering and squalor into enchantment. His friend Pulu invites him to go to a country wedding, and they make the trip lightheartedly, anticipating drink and revelry, music and horseplay and jokes. The bride, Aparna, played by Sarmila Tagore, who is lovely, is the daughter of a prosperous family. Dressed in her bridal costume, she awaits the arrival of her betrothed. But when he comes, he is mad; his head lolls and rolls crazily, his eyes are daft, and the wedding, of necessity, is off. The family faces a grave dilemma, for if Aparna is not married now that all the preparations have been made, she will be ostracized and will never be able to marry and will never be fulfilled. A substitute husband must be found: he is found in Apu.

For a year the couple live rapturously in Apu's dismal digs in Calcutta, and at the end of that time Aparna returns to her parents to be delivered of her child. Her death in childbed sends Apu into an enraged frenzy of grief, and his hatred

of his son, who killed her, is murderous. After several years of struggle and despair and loneliness, Apu at last goes to his father-in-law's house to meet the boy for the first time. Making friends with the shy, wild Kajol is not easy, but eventually the two are reconciled and the picture ends with the two going down a road, the son astride his father's shoulders. They are on their way to share, in familial love, the monotonous life of hunger and disease lived by millions of Indians, resigned to hell on earth.

I have heard that this monumental work was not well received in India, where the taste of the cinema-goers is for sweet love stories and sentimental musicals. In a way, I don't wonder. Why pay to see on the screen the same misery one has seen in the streets on the way to the theater? But to a Western audience, it is a profound lesson.

The World of Apu struck me as very much more moving and dramatic than *Aparajito,* but I remain convinced that *Pather Panchali* was the best. It would be interesting to see all three consecutively to determine the ways in which Ray has varied and developed his technique. The photography in all is immaculate, the details in all are scrupulously true. But there is not the same consistency of tension nor is there the same kind of acting. The acting in the first was flawless; in the last, Soumitra Chatterjee, as Apu, frequently disconcerted me with what I can only, regretfully, call his mugging. A year or so ago Indian friends who had seen *The World of Apu* at the Venice Film Festival told me that this was the masterpiece; perhaps the overstatement of emotion is what Indian intellectuals admire in an actor.

My complaints are minor. Ray has given us a masterpiece.

—JEAN STAFFORD

BOOKS

Beer–bottle on the Pediment

The thought of what America would be like
If the Classics had a wide circulation
Troubles my sleep.

So, in one of those formless and arrogant utterances that he called poems, wrote Ezra Pound. He meant it to be a hostile criticism of his native country, as a land of boors. But a thoughtful reader might interpret the sentence differently. If the classics of Greece and Rome really had a wide circulation in the United States, Pound would long ago have been not only despised as a traitor and pitied as a lunatic but unmasked as a charlatan.

Born in 1885, Ezra Pound left his native country in 1908 and in time was forgotten by his contemporaries. But recent critics have been treating him with respect. Mr. Charles Norman has given us his biography (*Ezra Pound*, Macmillan, 1960), and Mr. M. L. Rosenthal, an introduction to his poetry (*A Primer of Ezra Pound*, Macmillan, 1960). Nearly all that is written in this country about his poetry is respectful, even enthusiastic. There is an *Annotated Index to the* (first eighty-four) *Cantos of Ezra Pound*, compiled with impressive self-sacrifice by Messrs. J. H. Edwards and W. W. Vasse (University of California Press, 1957), who observe in their prefatory note that "the poem, like the mountain, was there." However, Pound's *Cantos* are not Everest. They are a dump containing some beautiful fragments of antique and Oriental sculpture (often disfigured by careless handling), some outrageous fakes, loads of personal trivia, some bits of filth, many promising but embryonic artistic sketches, and a huge scree of pure rubbish.

Pound always made a great show of learning and a bold claim to authority. His major work, the *Cantos*, is nearly as polyglot as Joyce's *Ulysses*. It contains sentences or phrases not only in poetic English (and slang both American and Cockney) but in Chinese, ancient Greek, classical and medieval Latin, French, Italian, Provençal, German, and jargons of various origin. Several of his books bear titles in Latin and other tongues: *Lustra, A Lume Spento, Personae*. One claims to be a translation or paraphrase of a difficult Latin poet, *Homage to Sextus Propertius*. His *Literary Essays* contain several boldly magisterial pronouncements—"Early Translators of Homer," "Notes on Elizabethan Classicists"—which look at first sight like products of serious scholarship. He even published a selection and discussion of Great Books called *How to Read*.

His interest in Greek and Latin is not merely a pose. It is an essential part of his development as a poet. Not only in using many different languages do his *Cantos* resemble Joyce's *Ulysses*. Both books are inspired by Greek poetry and myth: in particular by the myth of Odysseus as told by Homer. Joyce's Dedalus and Bloom are Prince Telemachus and King Odysseus modernized and debased. Pound, in the first of his *Cantos*, speaks through the mask of Odysseus, which he puts on at intervals thereafter. Mr. Rosenthal explains that Pound enriched that legend by crossing it with the myth of Dionysus, the god of ecstatic intoxication who was an adventurous traveler and a versatile lover and who, like Odysseus, often disguised himself; and Mr. Norman makes it clear that as the first Canto comes from Homer, so the second refers back to Ovid's *Metamorphoses*, a Roman poem on Greek mythical themes.

Now, to most of Pound's public, all this is impressive: especially when he throws in a few words of Greek or paraphrases a Latin poem or says something unintelligible but vaguely classical, like

this from Canto LXIV:

SUBILLAM

Cumis ego occulis meis
sleeping under a window: pray for me,
withered to skin and nerves tu theleis
respondebat illa
apothanein; pray for me gentlemen.

An earnest reader, who has no Greek or Latin himself, is pleasantly mystified and feels a vague admiration for a poet with so many strange echoes ringing in his mind. Most of his commentators treat Pound's intellectual equipment with deferential respect. Even if—like Mr. Norman—they decry his economic theorizing and detest his politics, they usually assume that, in poetry at least, he knows what he is talking about. They put in much hard work on tracing the sources of his allusions, classical and other; and often—as do Messrs. Edwards and Vasse—they tacitly correct what they take to be mere misprints and gently pass over the irrelevant and the inexplicable as though they were dark poetic mysteries. Critics in general seem to believe that Pound is a truly scholarly writer. How deeply, how accurately, and how sensitively he knows other languages I cannot tell; but he shows off his Greek and his Latin, although his Latin is poor and his Greek is contemptible.

What does this matter? Is it even true? Does not Pound's biographer, Mr. Norman, call the *Cantos* "an anthology of many literatures, quoted in the original . . . or translated by Pound with his incomparable skill?"

Unfortunately for an ambitious and energetic poet, it *is* true. Pound never had more than a smattering of Greek, scarcely enough to let him spell Greek words correctly either in the Greek alphabet or in our own. In Latin he knew enough to let him follow the general sense of a simple sentence and to grasp some of the more obvious effects of sound and rhythm, but not enough to permit him to understand or even to approach the greatest Roman poets or to save him from making coarse antipoetic blunders in interpreting Roman poetry. Worse than that, he would not learn. He would not admit his deficiencies and cure them through humility and industry. Nor would he avoid those areas where a display of ignorance would be damaging. Where others would turn their eyes away from the sanctuary, or else enter with quiet step and bowed head, Ezra Pound charged in, shouting and hiccuping, on roller skates, and rollicked around breaking the decorations and scrawling his name on the walls.

We see this in the opening pages of his most ambitious work. There he makes it clear that one of his chief personae, or masks, is to be Odysseus, and one of his chief themes the visit to the underworld. The opening Canto is a translation (with a few omissions) of the first 150 lines of the eleventh book of Homer's *Odyssey*. It is not a rethinking of the *Odyssey*, with its events and ideas transmuted and rearranged, nor even a loose paraphrase. It is a version which tries to be a close translation, sentence for sentence, sometimes line for line.

From time to time Pound's translation of the *Odyssey* becomes paradoxical or meaningless. If we are convinced that poetry, to be truly modern, must be paradoxical or meaningless, then we shall welcome certain passages. But if we remember that Pound was working on the clear narrative of a brilliantly lucid poet, we shall realize that he was not writing truly modern poetry but simply putting down words without sense. Thus, sailing from Circe's island, Odysseus reaches the fog-shrouded land of the Cimmerians, which Pound so describes:

The Kimmerian lands, and peopled cities
Covered with close-webbed mist, unpierced ever
With glitter of sun-rays
Nor with stars stretched, nor looking back from heaven
Swartest night stretched over wretched men there.

You might puzzle long over "Nor with stars stretched" before concluding that Homer meant the mist was never pierced by the sun nor thinned by starlight. You would be wrong, though it would be a logical interpretation. But you could never discover the meaning of "nor looking back from heaven," because it has no meaning. What Homer says is far more orderly and intelligible:

The sun looks never through the canopy of cloud,
either ascending up towards the starry heaven
or yet descending back from heaven towards the earth,
but deadly darkness stretches over the wretched folk.

Pound missed the central idea—that although the sun moves over the whole world, its rays never pierce the Cimmerian fogs from any angle; and so he wrote a sentence which was not only silly but (with its repetition of "stretched" in two different senses and its hideous echo "stretched . . . wretched") unpoetical.

The very next sentence is inexplicable:

The ocean flowing backward, came we then to the place
Aforesaid by Circe.

If the ocean flowed backward—presumably in a gigantic tidal wave—why was Odysseus's ship unaffected? Or was this a sinister deviation in the current off the land of the dead? It was not. The Greeks thought the ocean was a great salt stream flowing all round the world; Odysseus said, "We followed along the stream of Ocean" (presumably into the cold north), and Pound got it wrong.

And so it goes throughout Canto I. The stream of meaning keeps flowing backward, because Pound is an inveterate, but unlucky, guesser. Odysseus meets the ghost of one of his sailors who died because he got drunk, slept it off on the roof, and missed the ladder coming down. Pound makes him say, "I slept in Circe's ingle," which means the cosy fireside corner from which nobody could possibly fall down and break his neck.

You will wonder how a presumably sensitive writer could so grossly misrepresent the thoughts of a greater poet. If Pound had not been endeavoring to follow Homer closely, if he had been writing, as it were, free variations on a theme, these alterations of tone and meaning would have been understandable. But he was obviously trying to put Homer exactly into his own style of English. Now, if a more modest or more dedicated poet did not know Greek and yet wished to use a passage from Homer in his poetry, he would take five or six versions of Homer in languages which he understood—English, French, and Italian, for instance—and by combining them and extracting their essence, he might come fairly close to the original. Or—reflecting that art is long—he would set out to learn Greek. Pound did neither. He used a line-for-line, word-for-word translation from Homer's Greek into flat literal Latin prose which was published in 1538 by a hack named Andrea Divo. Whether he thought this was the best available translation, it is difficult to tell. If he did, he was quite wrong. In any case, the affectation of using a Renaissance Latin pony for a Greek poem caused him more trouble than it was worth. Not only did Andrea Divo sometimes get Homer's meaning wrong, but Ezra Pound sometimes got Andrea Divo's meaning wrong. The result was a double layer of misunderstanding spread, like Cimmerian cloud, between the radiant sun of Homer and Pound's wretched readers beneath.

Now, these are not trivial or pedantic criticisms. They go to the heart of Pound's poetic ambitions. He opens his central work by translating Homer: that is, by putting himself into competition, or close connection, with one of the greatest poets in the world. If a French poet began his major poem with an extract from *Paradise Lost* turned into French, he would be asking for equally severe criticism. Dante, though following Vergil with loving devotion, nevertheless translates only a few short passages directly from Vergil, and those into a different but more lucid style. Pound takes Homer's brisk, clear narrative and makes it a halting monologue studded with wrongheaded and meaningless phrases, like the ramblings of a medium or the reminiscences of an alcoholic.

And he finishes this, the exordium of his ambitious autobiography, with five lines of pure gibberish—mixed Latin and English—which have nothing whatever to do with the subject and are simply stuck on like a random collage because he cannot think how to conclude his first Canto. Leafing through the Latin translation he had been using, he found, following the *Odyssey*, a line-for-line prose translation of the Homeric hymns made by a Greek from Crete. His eye fell on the short second hymn to Aphrodite. From its opening he copied and translated a few disjointed words and phrases and jammed them into this hotchpotch:

> *Venerandam,*
> *In the Cretan's phrase, with the golden crown, Aphrodite,*
> *Cypri munimenta sortita est, mirthful, oricalchi, with golden*
> *Girdles and breastbands, thou with dark eyelids*
> *Bearing the golden bough of Argicida.*

This is not poetry but confetti. "Girdles and breastbands" is rubbish and shows the cheapness of Pound's mind. The Graces would not dress the new goddess Aphrodite in a girdle and brassière: Aphrodite has no need of such things. They gave her "a crown and necklaces." Nor were her radiant young eyelids "dark." Her Greek worshiper said she had "glancing eyes," moving quickly and softly like light on water. The Renaissance translator called them "liquid eyelids" (*enigras*, a misspelling of a rare Greco-Latin word, *enhygras*). Pound naturally missed this; he ignored the original Greek, which was much easier to understand, and misconceived the whole picture, making young Aphrodite into a vulgar mascara-laden vamp. To top it off, he gave her a golden bough, which she never carried, and attributed it to "Argicida," the Slayer of Argus, a title of the god Hermes which he found in a hymn several pages earlier and which could not be more out of place. Last of all, Aphrodite, the bright goddess of love and beauty, is logically and poetically irrelevant to Odysseus and his dark visit to the world of the dead. This is pure fakery: a meager pretense of learning, cynically manipulated to look like the product of deep knowledge and intense poetic imagination.

It would be easy to expand these charges against Pound as a poet and an interpreter of poets. His *Homage to Sextus Propertius* is an insult both to poetry and to scholarship, and to common sense. It consists of twelve free-verse poems which try to follow, very closely, the themes and wording of certain love elegies by Propertius. On every page Pound displays his ignorance, as though confident that, for scholars, his verse will be too subtle, and, for amateurs, his knowledge of foreign tongues will be overpowering. But he can grasp neither the important little details nor the large essentials; and the suave and delicate rhythms of Propertius's poetry are quite beyond his grasp.

The Latin love-word for a sweetheart is *puella*. Kinder than *domina*, it can describe another man's wife or an unmarried woman or a courtesan, provided the poet is tenderly and passionately in love with her and she reciprocates or may soon reciprocate. The word is used in this sense only in love poetry and similar genres: not in high poetry or dignified prose. It is a diminutive: so *mea puella* is "my girl" in modern English. Even this simple central fact about Latin love poetry is hidden from Pound: he makes *puella* now into "woman," which is insensitive, and now into "young lady," which is pompous and absurd.

As for his larger misinterpretations, one out of many will show their quality. In an important poem dealing with his own mission, Propertius says that being a poet of love, he cannot write epic poetry. He then runs through some famous heroic themes: the Trojan War, Xerxes' invasion of Greece, the ambitions of Carthage, and "the challenges of the Cimbrians and the good deeds of Marius." He means the formidable attack upon Italy by the Germanic tribe of the Cimbrians, ending in their defeat by the Roman general Marius. What does Pound do with this? He makes Propertius say that he cannot write "of Welsh coal-mines and the profit Marus had out of them." This is ingenious rubbish. The Romans did not mine coal and had not then penetrated into Wales. Pound, like a sophomore, wanted to give a bright answer quickly, without thinking. He remembered that the Welsh call themselves "Cymry," and "challenges" in Latin is *minas*, so *Cimbrorum minas* became "Welsh coal-mines," and "the good deeds of Marius" was vulgarized into "the profits of Marus." The misinterpretation of Propertius's words is disgusting but explicable and even, from some points of view, amusing. What is more disgusting is that Pound, himself a poet, should have so degraded the sen-sitive thoughts of another poet. Propertius gracefully explained that he could not handle epic themes and listed the noblest. Pound made him say that he could not discuss a mineowner's dividends—a subject far from high poetry and far beneath Propertius's attention and utterly irrelevant. This is not a mistake in language. It is a fundamental failure of taste.

Reflecting on Pound's incoherent and shallow work, reading the record of his painfully wasted life, glancing through the respectful but impercipient commentaries on his poems, we can understand why many intelligent people—not only in the United States but elsewhere in the civilized world—turn away from him with pity and scorn. He ruined what might have been a viable talent because he believed that he could be a great writer without humility, without knowledge, and without concentration. When he began to write, he possessed several of the qualities of a poet. His mistake was to believe that he was already complete, and that these few qualities were enough. In Canto LXXIV he quoted the Greek proverb "Beauty is difficult"; but he did not remember it. He wrecked his mind with exhibition and competition and improvisation and opposition and destructive criticism and silly self-advertisement and pointless correspondence and a perpetual compulsive self-justificatory monologue which served as a substitute for thought. And there was always a regrettable cheapness and crudity in Pound's talk and writing, which is politely alluded to in Mr. Norman's biography and which makes several of his Cantos not only unreadable but unprintable. When, recalling a conversation with a friend, he wrote: "Beer-bottle on the statue's pediment! That, Fritz, is the era, to-day against the past," he was unconsciously describing the effect of his own poetry: a shiny brittle vulgarity posing as a classical work of art. And in his version of Propertius he summed up his own chances of fame:

> *"I shall have, doubtless, a boom after my funeral,*
> *Seeing that long standing increases all things*
> *regardless of quality."*

—GILBERT HIGHET

ADVERTISING

The Sad End of the Word "Fabulous"

It is now possible to report, with some satisfaction, that the use of the word "fabulous" in advertising copy is down 8.6 per cent from 1959–60 and is to be found in a mere 64.7 per cent of all advertisements. This may not seem impressive, but it must be realized that in 1956–57 the corresponding figure was 99.87 per cent, and rising. If the present trend continues, by 1980 or so that particular adjective will be reserved for advertisers seeking to move large stocks of unicorns and gryphons; on the other hand, some equally inane adjective will no doubt have taken its place.

It all began, I suspect, with the superb popular song "Just One of Those Things." Cole Porter had jotted down as a first approximation:

> *It was just one of those nights,*
> *Just one of those Dum-di-dum*
> *flights . . .*

And right in there he needed a DUM-di-dum word beginning with *f*. Such words are lamentably few, but in time he came upon "fabulous" and chucked it in. (I have not submitted this hypothesis to Mr. Porter for verification and do not intend to.) "Fabulous," if it means anything, signifies "as found in fables," and while I don't recall any fable dealing with trips to the moon on gossamer wings, the notion is surely within reach of the imagination. This is a good deal more than can be said about a tooth paste that has a "fabulous new ingredient."

An advertisement frequently cries out for words that don't mean a thing, like "sensational" or "milder." (Note that the word "mild" *does* mean something and accordingly is never seen. Just "milder.") What bothers me is that it doesn't sound very good, either. Reduced to guesswork about its meaning, one would tend to use it in a sentence like "His upper plate having worked loose, he was reduced to speaking fabulously." Words that are used as "fabulous" is commonly used—simply to make a noise—should at least sound good. Children's names, for example, are merely noise-words, and I once threw all my support behind a friend who wanted to name his daughter "Tawdry." He thought it sounded fine, and so do I. But his wife created a scene, and the poor girl is named Karen, as indeed who is not?

But I seem to have wandered from my subject, whatever it was. It was not grammar, by the way. I was never one of those who objected to "Winston tastes good, like a cigarette should"—as a locution, that is. It is clear, unambiguous, reasonably harmonious, and exactly what any normal American would say, assuming he was moved to say anything at all about Winstons. Abnormal persons, like magazine editors, who might very well say *"as* a cigarette should," smoke pipes, which they rub against their noses to bring out the grain. English grammar is arbitrary and chaotic and suffers from a long history of pedantic misapprehension: for centuries it was stubbornly taught under the impression that it was Latin. Any changes made by people who actually use the language are likely to be changes for the better.

The English vocabulary is something else again. Words are our basic means of communication. No two words convey precisely the same message; every word has its own job to do, and we need it. To seize upon a word, and by constant misuse to rob it of all meaning, is to impoverish the language for us all. I don't mind so much about "fabulous"—I wasn't using it a lot anyway—but I am worried about the next word that is to be bastardized by my friends on Madison Avenue. It may be a word we need, like "bastardized."

All this is discouraging and leaves me no recourse but to leaf through the pages of *The New Yorker,* where any concept, notion, or adjective that has already been used seven times is automatically barred. *The New Yorker* is far too smart for that sort of thing. *The New Yorker,* in fact, is as smart as a magazine can possibly be and still circulate outside the immediate family. Of course, that also has its risks. Consider, for example, a recent advertisement which displays, over three-fourths of its space, a man, nondescript in every respect, seated on a camel in an attitude of extreme discomfort and reading a copy of *Punch.* On the camel are printed the words "Hose, too, of course." The copy then goes on to say:

BIG MAN ON CAMEL

—as seen in Punch

"Effendi!" cried our Assistant Master Stylist in a voice too loud, "Stanley is dead!" AMS is really a decent fellow and a superb stylist, but (unlike our Master Stylist whom we lost several generations ago, rest his soul) unfortunately given to hyperbole. When we had removed his turban and cooled his brow, we learned that he had merely conceived a new sweater at once so comfortable and so splendidly correct for lounging that it stood a distinct chance of displacing the Stanley Kowalski look in campi and suburbs.

It goes on like that, smart to the point of hysteria. I get the impression that they are trying to tell me something, but there must be easier ways. It might even be a relief if they simply said that their camel's-hair sweaters are fabulous, absolutely fabulous. You can't win.

—STEPHEN WHITE

A HISTORY OF ART By MICHAEL THALER

In the darkness of a cave a brave spirit took a brand from the fire and drew upon the walls—setting himself apart from the animals. Art was born. Not quite understood by his fellows, made to stand in a corner, the artist nonetheless developed. Innovator and experimenter, he divined the perfection of certain forms and re-created the shapes of the world surrounding him.

THE BEGINNING

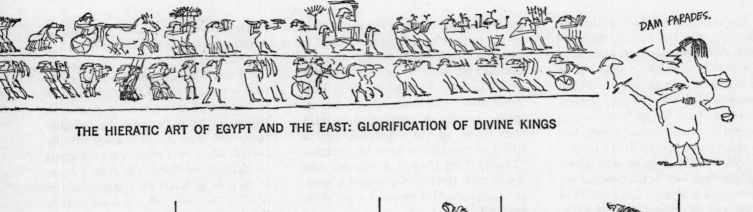

THE HIERATIC ART OF EGYPT AND THE EAST: GLORIFICATION OF DIVINE KINGS

GREECE AND ROME: IDEALIZATION OF THE HUMAN FORM

THE MIDDLE AGES: A SINGLENESS OF PURPOSE

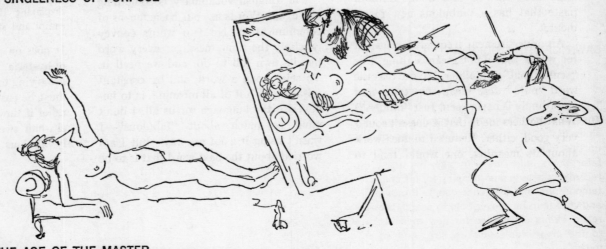

THE RENAISSANCE: THE AGE OF THE MASTER

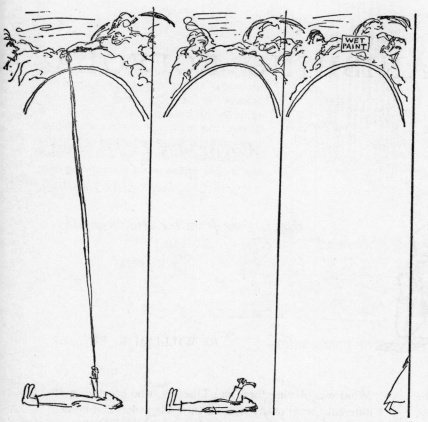

THE HIGH RENAISSANCE: ONWARD AND UPWARD WITH THE ARTS

BAROQUE—ROCOCO: OPULENCE AND SENSUALITY

THE ROMANTIC AGE: REVOLUTION AND BOURGEOISIE, THE ARTIST AS SPOKESMAN

DAWN OF THE MODERN MOVEMENT: ART FOR ART'S SAKE, THE STARVING ARTIST

Thus has man fashioned the many mansions of the house of art. Consciously or unconsciously the reflector and commentator of his milieu in every age, the artist records its beauty and meaning for his contemporaries and his successors. Prophet and voyageur, he is ever bold to search the realm of his experience for new meaning to the great riddles before him. And so today . . .

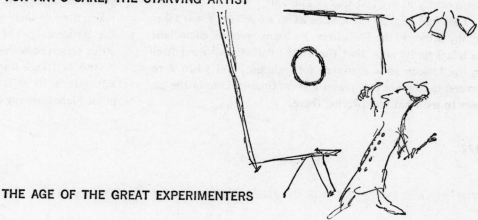

THE AGE OF THE GREAT EXPERIMENTERS

THE VANISHING BOFFOLA

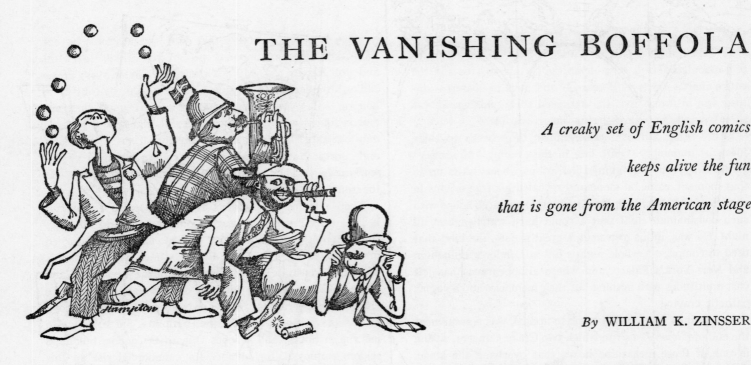

A creaky set of English comics

keeps alive the fun

that is gone from the American stage

By WILLIAM K. ZINSSER

Of all the ancient monuments in London none impressed me so much for sheer durability, not even Westminster Abbey, as a sextet of vaudeville comics known collectively as "The Crazy Gang." The fact that their individual names contain in two places the character &—they are Nervo & Knox, Bud Flanagan, Naughton & Gold, and "Monsewer" Eddie Gray —suggests that they are an agglomeration of old variety acts, as indeed they have been for thirty years, and the fact that one of them bears the cognomen "Monsewer" is a fair index to their group taste in humor.

They are said to be the favorite entertainers of the Royal Family, which doesn't bode too well for the monarchy, if true—and it probably is, for when I saw their revue, *Clown Jewels*, a photograph of Queen Elizabeth smiled ecstatically down on her subjects from a wall in the theater lobby. And yet I think I understand, if a mere commoner may make such surmises, what it is about the six buffoons that the Queen finds so diverting.

At the time of my visit last spring, *Clown Jewels* had been running, at two shows nightly, for six hundred performances, and I expected lines of fatigue to be etched deeply on its corporate brow. Friends had warned me that a few pre-theater drinks would make the evening bearable, if not necessarily enjoyable, and though I took the precaution of following their advice, bourbon was only half responsible for the glow of anticipation with which I settled into my seat at a quarter to nine o'clock. I was also making a pilgrimage to the memory of my last trip to London.

That had been in 1939, when as an adolescent I was taken by my father to the Palladium. So funny were its comedians, so hilarious its acts, that the word "Palladium" fixed itself in my lexicon as a synonym for paradise, and when I returned to London last year I lost no time looking in the papers to see what was playing there.

What was playing there was Liberace, who occupies quite a different corner of my lexicon. On asking what had become of vaudeville, I learned that it has almost completely vanished from England and that the hallowed Palladium is now inhabited by ordinary mortals—crooners, drummers, and such. So I went in desperation to the Crazy Gang, hoping to find in them some flickering spark of the enchanted past.

In appearance, at least, they fitted the classic image. Four of them reminded me, by a pleasant coincidence, of the great Bert Lahr, Bobby Clark, Victor Moore, and Groucho Marx. The other two reminded me of Olsen & Johnson, and as it soon turned out, the spiritual kinship of all six was closest to those two knockabouts, who shepherded *Hellzapoppin'* across America for what seemed like a solid decade, if not eternity.

Old age had overtaken them. Flanagan, who appeared before one backdrop that said "Born 1896 and Still Going Wrong," was probably the youngest. The others had reached that autumnal stage where potbellies rest ludicrously on skinny white legs—a condition not noticeable in most trades that old men practice, but hard to conceal in clowns who frequently lose their trousers or dress up as girls.

Both these routines were staples of the Crazy Gang's repertory. At one point they turned up as debutantes being presented at Buckingham Palace and looking quite grotesque —especially one dotard who was well into his seventies and who, as we were later informed, had just been married. His probable debility as a bridegroom lent itself to four or five jokes, none of them subtle (several were built on allusions to the Battersea power plant); for the Crazy Gang were not strict believers in the purity of the spoken word.

And yet there was a certain innocence about their show, not only in its skits but in its production numbers. At one point Flanagan sang a ballad called "Strollin'" which, though new, had the period flavor of "In the Good Old Summertime" or "Bicycle Built for Two." It extolled the pleasures of a moonlight stroll, whereupon the curtains parted and the entire chorus—girls with parasols and boys in boaters—ambled arm in arm across the darkened stage, singing. It was so naïve and unabashed that it was irresistible.

Many other numbers were similar throwbacks to early forms of mummery. Quite late in the evening "Monsewer" Eddie Gray, who had figured in various wheezy skits up to that moment, came on alone and revealed his true origins in show business. He manipulated a half-dozen large hoops with such consummate skill that I could have watched him all night. He was, in his own field, a great artist—the kind that used to comprise a whole night's bill in London's Palladium and New York's Palace, and whose disappearance has left vast multitudes with nothing but their memories and a vague, pathetic craving.

Less refined, but equally basic in appeal, was a scene near the end of *Clown Jewels* in which two Crazy Gangers, sitting in one of those mezzanine boxes that overhang the stage, threw oranges at their colleagues below, pelting them when their backs were turned and sometimes, with surprising accuracy, knocking their hats off. Between throws they all exchanged a great deal of banter which, by any standards of humor, was a long way from being good. But the two comedians in the box were so convulsed by what they were saying and doing (though they had done it earlier that very night and six-hundred-odd times before) that they could hardly speak their lines, and again I was swept along in the contagion of the event.

For one thing, I am a sucker for the simple humor of the flying object, or even of the wielded object. Let one baggypants clown hit another with a bladder, for instance, and I will be in a seizure of joy. But what really delighted me about the scene, and about *Clown Jewels* as a whole, was that its six old men were so endearingly eager to please the audience and so easily pleased themselves. Whatever burlesque talents they may once have had were now rusted over; their voices were almost as scratchy as their jokes. But they had never lost, in the hundreds of years and countless thousands of nights that their careers encompassed, their fresh enthusiasm for comedy's oldest tools.

The fact that they used these tools poorly didn't bother me. I laughed throughout, at times uncontrollably, and so did the capacity audience. I laughed partly because some gags were funny, and partly because some were so terrible, but mostly because I was having a good time. I was being offered pure entertainment—a commodity that an American can hardly get in his own country any more, unless Danny Kaye is at large or unless he has access to the silent films of Mack Sennett, Buster Keaton, Laurel & Hardy, and other masters of the visual joke.

For humor has largely gone out of our arts, and where it does survive it is seldom humor for its own sake. The nation now takes itself so seriously that even its jokes must have a point, and our most honored wits are those like Mort Sahl and Bob Newhart, or Mike Nichols and Elaine May, whose sallies are edged with meaning. They should, of course, be honored—they are brilliant, and we need them. If their humor is somewhat "sick," these are sick times, and perhaps only our satirists and parodists can help us see the malaise and cure it. But when we laugh at comics like Sahl we are working hard. They require of us a mental effort and a taste for irony.

There remains the problem, also important to a country's health, of making people laugh spontaneously, and the practitioners of this art are nearly extinct. Chaplin has turned into other paths. The Marx Brothers have closed up shop. W. C. Fields and Bobby Clark are dead. Bert Lahr and Nancy Walker languish for lack of material. Danny Kaye limits his appearances. Jerry Lewis doesn't, but ought to—he has the instincts but not the discipline. Sid Caesar also has the instincts; and so does Donald O'Connor, but he is seldom employed, for humor is a commercial risk in this land of the renowned sense of humor.

Fun and farce have been gone from Broadway for many seasons—the theater is in a gloomy and introverted mood, and even our good musicals, such as *West Side Story, Fiorello,* and *The Sound of Music,* unfold to contrapuntal themes of crime, politics, and war. Broadway could use, heretical as this may seem in the era of "integrated" musicals, a few grab-bag shows—like George White's *Scandals* or Ziegfeld's *Follies*—whose aim is simply to amuse the audience and whose songs do not advance the plot because there is no plot to advance.

Funny movies come along once a year, if we are lucky, and we are pitifully thankful to the men who create them. Billy Wilder, probably Hollywood's wittiest craftsman, basked in the gratitude of the populace—and in huge profits —for writing and directing *Some Like It Hot.* Its mere presence in the movie houses of America brought pleasant echoes of the years when Hollywood gave us a steady diet of comedies, like *It Happened One Night, The Awful Truth, The Thin Man, The Great McGinty,* and—well, anybody over thirty can name dozens. But Wilder is also a moralist, and his film *The Apartment,* though frequently droll, has such sardonic overtones that a movie-goer doesn't really know whether to laugh or cry. Thus even our movie comedies have lost their essential gaiety.

It is time for the boff and the belly laugh to be heard in the land again. Let bladders resound and prats fall, let top bananas grow on trees. Let some poor Pantaloon tumble into the bass drum or into a bin of flour; let him even—I am this desperate—see pie in the sky, headed for him. Let some impresario mount a full evening of vaudeville, bringing "Monsewer" Eddie Gray and his hoops from London and leaving his jokes behind. If this be treason, I can always move to England. It's anything but *lèse-majesté* over there.

THE SECRETS OF SAN MEN

TEXT CONTINUED FROM PAGE II

laces of carnelian (previously unknown in Chinese burials), the distribution of other jade rings called *pi* in more or less precise order over the funerary wrappings of the noble, double wooden coffins surmounted by the curious *ko* (an abstract shape in stone, patterned with dissolved animal motifs). All these features were nearly constant. Only thirty-eight of the tombs contained bronzes, but among those were the unique *tou* (a vessel in the shape of a cup borne by a fantastic animal and probably used for wine—page 4) as well as the earliest Chinese bronze mirrors decorated with figures of birds and beasts. Lacquered wooden bowls and dishes had survived their long burial remarkably well; their jet-black and Chinese-red decoration was still fresh, though the wood was very warped. One tomb contained two daggers which were dated and inscribed "Crown Prince Yuan T'u of Kuo."

Of the three chariot pits, the largest contained ten chariots and twenty horses, while the others had half as many of each. The better preserved of the smaller pits fortunately proved to belong to the Prince Yuan T'u and was close by his tomb. This burial is presently preserved *in situ* since the contents are too fragile to be moved. It is a remarkable experience to enter the low building over the pit and see, in the long rectangle ten feet below, those five princely chariots and their ten skeletal horses just as they were driven twenty-seven centuries ago (see page 8). There is even the skeleton of a small dog, which perhaps had run in and been inadvertently sealed up with the horses. The nature of the soil, and probably the excellent drainage in this particular spot, has preserved the chariots so perfectly that fine measurements can be made and the details of their construction discerned.

The importance of this find is that the chariots of Kuo appear to be the missing link, in the evolution of the Chinese war chariot, between those of Western Chou which were discovered at Sian and those of the later Eastern Chou period which were excavated in Honan.

In preliminary analysis the excavations at Shang Ts'un Ling yield a well-documented picture of life and culture in what was formerly a vacuum between Western and Eastern Chou times. The dating is exact, and the objects are so many and so complete that they afford the opportunity to reassess all the other information we possess concerning the Chou Dynasty. From the historical viewpoint it now seems possible to clarify further this turbulent era when the Chinese feudalism that was to endure for more than two thousand years emerged from primitive village commune systems.

When I returned to San Men in 1959, I found to my dismay that the astonishing view of the gorge had disappeared behind a wall of concrete bristling with men and machines. The two islands, for so long subjects of the myths of a traditional way of life, had themselves at last departed into the realms of mythology.

The waters of the lake will soon rise and erase the history still written in the yellow earth. For perhaps only 5 per cent of the possible prehistoric sites (especially those which may be presumed to be the most primitive of the neolithic era and whatever went before it, and which doubtless lie closest to the banks of the river) have been excavated. The stupendous archaeological effort made by the Chinese, who threw almost all their trained personnel into the work at the earliest possible opportunity, has of course not been sufficient to uncover all the remains in the large area that will be inundated by the lake. But what has been accomplished has undoubtedly added at least one vital page to Chinese history and has provided numerous treasures for the museums of Communist China.

Fortunately, the relatively unimportant but delightful temple of Yü will not be lost. The waters will not reach it. In the autumn of 1959 it was still moldering up there above the unrecognizable scene at San Men. I felt there was a delicate irony in the fact that although its traditional function has finally been obviated by the damming of the Yellow River, the temple where the boatmen sought to propitiate the River Dragon will soon be restored to its former state.

Nigel Cameron is an English journalist who, although young in years, has become something of an Old China Hand. With photographer Brian Brake, he has made several trips through Asia. His book on China is titled The Chinese Smile.

STATEMENT REQUIRED BY THE ACT OF AUGUST 24, 1912, AS AMENDED BY THE ACTS OF MARCH 3, 1933, JULY 2, 1946, AND JUNE 11, 1960 (74 Stat. 208) SHOWING THE OWNERSHIP, MANAGEMENT, AND CIRCULATION OF HORIZON, published bi-monthly at New York, N. Y. for October 1, 1960.

1. The names and addresses of the publisher, editor, and managing editor are: Publisher, James Parton, Editor, Joseph J. Thorndike, Jr., Managing Editor, William Harlan Hale, all of 551 Fifth Avenue, New York 17, N. Y.

2. The owner is: American Horizon, Inc., 551 Fifth Avenue, New York 17, N. Y.; stockholders owning or holding 1 per cent or more of total amount of stock: American Heritage Publishing Co., Inc.; William Harlan Hale; Oliver O. Jensen; Joseph J. Thorndike, Jr., individually and as Trustee under Declaration of Trust for John Thorndike, dated 12/27/57, as Trustee under Declaration of Trust for Alan Thorndike, dated 12/27/57 and as Voting Trustee under Agreement, dated 2/6/59, for James Parton and Alexander Hehmeyer; all of 551 Fifth Avenue, New York 17, N. Y.

3. The known bondholders, mortgagees, and other security holders owning or holding 1 per cent or more of total amount of bonds, mortgages, or other securities are: None.

4. Paragraphs 2 and 3 include, in cases where the stockholder or security holder appears upon the books of the company as trustee or in any other fiduciary relation, the name of the person or corporation for whom such trustee is acting; also the statements in the two paragraphs show the affiant's knowledge and belief as to the circumstances and conditions under which stockholders and security holders who do not appear upon the books of the company as trustees, hold stock and securities in a capacity other than that of a bona fide owner.

5. The average number of copies of each issue of this publication sold or distributed, through the mails or otherwise, to paid subscribers during the 12 months preceding the date shown above was: 150,440.

Signed, James Parton, Publisher. Sworn to and subscribed before me this 12th day of September, 1960. [SEAL] Laurence P. Sweeney, Notary Public (my commission expires March 30, 1962).

LUDWIG'S DREAM CASTLES

CONTINUED FROM PAGE 42

plored the taste of his time, was inevitably influenced by it; and if one looks at photographs of Ludwig's contemporaries —Queen Victoria in a sitting room at Sandringham that looks like the Old Curiosity Shop, or Kaiser Wilhelm competing for the photographer's attention with a welter of elk heads, ancestral portraits, Biedermeier sofas, Gothic armchairs, lace curtains, Oriental rugs, antlers, Meissen vases, and palm trees—one finds Ludwig's apartments restful. Everything, down to the last toothbrush holder, was designed for the exact place where it still stands. Each room is so like the next that one comes away with a blurred impression of dazzle and splendor, in which only a few bits stand out clearly—the life-sized porcelain peacock, the upright Aeolian piano strewn with gold rococo squiggles, or the canopy above the King's worktable, lined with ermine from the coronation robe of Ludwig's cousin Otto of Greece (this is the sole example anywhere in Ludwig's décor of thrift, or making-do, and one wonders if he minded the secondhand ermine). Some of the paintings are on tapestry, to imitate Gobelin, and the subjects are mythological or allegorical—no German sagas here. Pastel portraits of Marie Antoinette, of Louis XIV, XV, and XVI, of Madame du Barry, Madame de Pompadour, and other French court figures bear identical bland, custardy expressions; it was the abstract idea of absolute monarchy that interested Ludwig, not nuances of personality.

By the time Linderhof was ready for Ludwig to live in, his manner of life was further than ever removed from reality. He arose at six or seven in the evening and had breakfast, dined at two hours past midnight, supped and retired at dawn. He liked to take his meals alone, but the table was usually set for three or four. Who were the unseen guests? Louis XIV was one, perhaps; a servant once came upon Ludwig saluting and talking to a statue of Louis XIV that stands in the main hallway of Linderhof. (Ludwig believed himself a spiritual heir of the Bourbons because his grandfather, Ludwig I, had been a godson of Louis XVI. He sometimes called Linderhof "Meicost Ettal," an anagram of *l'état c'est moi*.) Often the ghostly dinner would take place at Ludwig's *Tischlein-deck-dich*, a table copied from one at Versailles that could pop into view, fully spread, by means of machinery that boosted it through the floor. The kitchen had always to be ready for sudden changes in the royal appetite. Ludwig liked kingly-looking food—peacock, for instance, stuffed with forcemeat and truffles and served up with its head and tail feathers. He expected dishes like this to be on hand when he wanted them and thought nothing of advancing or retarding dinner without consideration of the cooks' nerves. Sometimes he would suddenly decide to dine on a perch amid the branches of a large lime tree in the garden; or in a mountain hut; or at the Schachen, a hunting lodge designed in a curious blend of Swiss chalet and Turkish kiosk; or in one of several outbuildings that he con-

structed on the Linderhof grounds—the Moorish kiosk, Hunding's Hut, or the Grotto.

Hunding's Hut (destroyed in 1945) was a replica in-the-round of a stage set for the first act of *Die Walküre*. In the middle was a living ash tree, pierced by a replica of Siegfried's sword. For the rest, there were a lot of antlers and bearskins, and when the King was in a jovial mood, he and a few favored courtiers would lie about dressed as early Teutons and drink mead out of horns. Game was their principal food; silver jugs in the shape of deer held cream for the coffee—which would doubtless have surprised Siegfried —and the salt and pepper shakers were shaped like little owls.

When the Teutonic mood was not upon him, Ludwig had a penchant for the Oriental. In 1867, at the Paris Exposition, he had bought a Moorish kiosk, the property of a bankrupt millionaire from Bohemia, and this was eventually set up at Linderhof. The kiosk was not particularly Moorish, having been conceived and built in Berlin of pressed zinc plaques. But Ludwig was enchanted with it and installed a throne in the shape of a huge zinc peacock, its tail feathers enameled and set with glittering Bohemian glass. Next to swans, peacocks were the favorite bird of the King, and he cherished a desire to be drawn about by peacocks harnessed to a small gilded car, as he had heard was done in ancient Persia; he even wrote to the incumbent Shah of Persia, asking for a shipment of sturdy peacocks along with training instructions. No peacocks arrived, but he enjoyed lolling on his peacock throne and drinking a *bowle* made by soaking violet roots in champagne, accompanied by *petits fours* and candied violets.

But of all the phantasmagoria at Linderhof, the Grotto is the strangest. The inspiration for the Grotto came partly from the Blue Grotto in Capri, partly from the Venus Grotto, where Tannhäuser drank the cup of oblivion, and partly from Ludwig's father's bathroom at Hohenschwangau. The latter had been hollowed out of the rock on which the castle stands; it was lit by a red light in the ceiling and was entered by pressing a secret spring in a slab of papier-mâché rock. Ludwig's artificial grotto at Linderhof opens in the same manner, but outdoes the paternal bathroom in almost every other way. It is several hundred feet long, fifty feet high, and is not made of rock at all, but of brick and iron clothed in canvas and cement to make them look like rocks and stalagmites. It also contains a lake, which the King sometimes swam in and sometimes rowed about on in a gilded, shell-shaped boat. A waterfall gurgles noisily down from the bogus rocks, and in Ludwig's day artificial waves could be whipped up on the lake's surface by means of a small machine. Dim, varicolored lights and a luminous rainbow were provided by the first electricity plant in Bavaria, erected on an adjacent slope, and twenty-five dynamos (then very recently invented). Back of the lake, a huge painting depicts Act I of

Tannhäuser and swarms of cherubs and fairies. The whole place must have seemed very recherché to the King, but to a modern eye it is unfortunately reminiscent of the Coney Island fun house.

But if the Grotto is ridiculous, Ludwig was occasionally capable of the sublime. And if he ever achieved a triumph of creative imagination, it was in choosing the site for the castle of Neuschwanstein. It stands among monumental gray crags, with snowy Alps above, a green plain below, and the lovely little jade-green lakes of Schwansee and Alpsee not far away. One wonders if, in building it, Ludwig did not set out to outdo his father, for the windows of this castle look down on Hohenschwangau, which in comparison is only the restored fortress of a petty lord. The architects of Neuschwanstein worked from sketches made by the same scene designer who worked on Linderhof, and probably no professional architect would have arrived at such a never-never look for solid stone- and brickwork. During the construction, Ludwig was often on hand to supervise the workmen personally; but the royal apartments took so long to build and decorate that in all he was only able to occupy them for less than half a year.

Unhappily, the castle interior is less felicitous than its exterior. Romanesque, Early Gothic, Late Gothic, Tudor, Moorish, and Byzantine architecture and decorations are chucked together with a heavy hand, and everywhere are those outsized insipid paintings that could only be nineteenth century. Tristan and Isolde, Lohengrin and Elsa, Walther and Eva, and other heroes and heroines of Middle High German poetry command the walls, looking noble, vacuous, and stiff as pokers. Never was so much love celebrated with so little reference to sex. In a painting showing Tannhäuser on the Venusberg, which dominates the King's study, Venus is as naked as, but no more sensual than, a billiard ball, while Tannhäuser, fully clothed, sits at her feet and looks as if he were thinking out a chess problem. Then there are the usual Ludwigian touches: a bathrooom full of artificial stalactites (what *was* this family passion for bathing in a cave?), a porcelain vase in the shape of a full-sized swan, and a carved oak bed-canopy in Late Gothic style that is a perfect forest of turrets, ogives, and pinnacles. Ludwig always gave most attention to the royal bedroom, which he regarded as a symbol of monarchy. Louis XIV had received courtiers, ministers, and sundry callers in bed, and Ludwig may have intended to copy him, but as he grew older he rarely received anyone. The last room added to Neuschwanstein was a throne room, which, like so much else in Ludwig's castles, was of no use at all. The theme is Byzantine, for more and more, Ludwig was drawn to the Byzantine concept of royalty as near-deity. The throne itself, which was to be of ivory and pure gold, never materialized; above the empty space reserved for it are murals—painted to resemble mosaic—depicting six canonized kings of Christendom and, above them, the risen Christ with Saint John and the Virgin, so that the room seems something like a church. This is the most the-atrical-looking of all Ludwig's rooms, perhaps because the paintings are faked mosaics and the pillars, supposed to look like porphyry and lapis lazuli, are too red and too blue and are obviously only plaster. By the time Ludwig planned the throne room, his sight was weakening, and, being a very vain man, he would not wear glasses; also, because of his peculiar schedule, he rarely saw anything by light brighter than candle or moon. At any rate, he must by this time have felt like a man who, by walking onto a stage set, has turned it into a real world, while the commonplace life of the pit and the stalls has faded forever into darkness and hush.

Ludwig's third *Schloss*, Herrenchiemsee, inspired by and partly copied from Versailles, stands on a small island in the Chiemsee, one of the largest of the Bavarian alpine lakes. The cornerstone was laid in 1878 and building continued, to the tune of twenty million marks, until 1885, when the state treasury put a stop to it, leaving some twenty rooms finished and sumptuously decorated and the rest of the palace no more than bare bricks and plaster. These royal rooms, lighted by thousands of white candles in more than a hundred crystal, ivory, or porcelain chandeliers, are an extraordinary sight, a sight that Ludwig is said to have seen only once, when he walked from room to room all alone. By day, when Ludwig never saw the palace, it looks gaudy and overdone and reminds one all too plainly how difficult it is for a man to escape his century. The great entrance hall is meticulously copied after the Ambassadors' Staircase at Versailles; yet the unsubtle colors of the ubiquitous heroic paintings, the staring-white stucco, and the disastrous idea of adding a glass roof (suggesting Waterloo Station), mark it inexorably as a work of the late nineteenth century. Dissatisfied with the empty appearance of Louis XIV's Hall of Mirrors, Ludwig supplied his version with 47 banquettes, 12 tabourets, 52 candelabras, 8 orange trees in specially designed tubs, 4 vases, 16 busts of classical emperors, and 33 chandeliers. The painted figures that swarm across the ceiling have been provided here and there with stucco legs and arms, which make them look as if they were wildly trying to struggle free of the ceiling. This whimsy of Bavarian eighteenth-century rococo would have dismayed a seventeenth-century Frenchman and imparts a slightly berserk appearance to this Hall of Mirrors.

Ludwig slept in his costly palace exactly nine nights, from September 7 to 16, 1885. He himself said that he had intended it less as a dwelling than a temple, a shrine dedicated to the Sun King, Louis XIV, and to the idea of Absolutism. The most important and most expensive room in the palace is the bedroom for the symbolic use of Louis XIV, modeled after the royal bedroom at Versailles but larger and far more elaborate. Ludwig supplied the ghost of his idol with a golden railing to separate the bed from the rest of the room—an old Bavarian idea, not French at all. He also gave Louis a gilt bowl and pitcher big enough for a giant, hangings of dark red velvet that took twenty women seven years to encrust with gold embroidery, a parquet floor intricately inlaid with rosewood, and a tapestry-painting showing Louis XIV with his ancestor Saint Louis and—unobtrusively standing in the background—his spiritual descendant, Ludwig.

Ludwig's own bedroom is comparatively modest. The draperies are blue, the color Ludwig preferred in all his bedrooms, and there is a giant blue globe at the foot of the bed to serve as a night light. Here, as in every bedroom he planned for himself, is a curious juxtaposition of religious and amorous symbols. At the head of the bed is an embroidery depicting Louis XIV triumphing over Vice, while at the foot is a carved relief of Venus set between fully modeled figures of Cupid and Psyche.

Although Herrenchiemsee was not nearly finished, Ludwig set about planning more castles. There was to be a Byzantine palace, a robber-baron eyrie on a higher and less accessible crag than Neuschwanstein, and a walled Chinese palace where the court was to adopt the dress and ceremonial of mandarins. There was one rather large stumbling block: money. The King's credit was no longer good anywhere, and he owed ten million marks. When a moneylender came forward with the offer of a four-hundred-thousand-mark loan in return for a title, Ludwig, though he eventually gave in, at first refused indignantly: Did they suppose the King had no honor? His advisers pleaded with him. Where else, they asked, could the money be found? "Steal it!" cried Ludwig.

Early in the morning of Thursday, June 10, 1886, a delegation of ministers of state, accompanied by a noted psychiatrist, Dr. Bernhard von Gudden, and several skilled male nurses, arrived at the gatehouse of Neuschwanstein. They brought with them a parliamentary order to place the King under medical care. There was a clause in the Bavarian constitution stating that a king incapable of carrying out his proper duties could be relieved of them and replaced by a regency; that Ludwig was incapable seemed so apparent that four psychiatrists, none of whom had ever seen the King, had signed a report declaring him insane. In addition to his unreasoning demands for money and his paralyzing effect on the orderly processes of government (when papers required the royal signature, ministers often had to meet the King in some remote mountain rendezvous where, in the middle of the night, Ludwig would arrive by coach-and-six, hurriedly sign the papers with his now illegible "Ludwig," and whirl away again), there was a stack of evidence obtained from his servants: that they must approach the King on their bellies, that he had them physically chastised and bound, that he talked to trees and embraced a certain pillar at Linderhof each time he passed it, and that he complained of terrible pressure in his head, sometimes so severe that he had to come to meals wearing an ice pack.

The members of the commission from Munich had not brought military support with them, and, to their annoyance,

they found that the King's loyal guard would not let them into Neuschwanstein. There was nothing for them to do but withdraw to the nearest village and wonder what to do next. They had not long to wonder: within the hour a company of gendarmes arrived from the King with orders to arrest them. In vain they showed the captain of gendarmes a paper stating that Prince Luitpold, the King's uncle, was already Regent; finally they consented to the indignity of being locked up in the Neuschwanstein gatehouse. The King now issued a series of five orders that at last shook the faith of his supporters. The orders were (1) skin the members of the commission alive, (2) scalp them, cut off their tongues and hands, and flog them to death, (3) blind them, (4) place them in heavy chains, and (5) fling them into a deep dungeon to starve to death. Afterwards the captain of gendarmes admitted that if the royal order had simply directed him to shoot all members of the commission, he would unhesitatingly have carried it out. As it was, he and his assistants debated for several hours before deciding to try to get instructions from the government in Munich.

Before all the red tape had been cut and Dr. Gudden was finally free to try to take charge of his patient, two more days had passed, and Ludwig was drinking heavily, threatening suicide, and calling for the keys to the highest tower of Neuschwanstein. Dr. Gudden stationed the male nurses on the tower stairway and then had the keys sent to Ludwig. Ludwig immediately made for the tower, was taken, and then driven in a locked carriage to the small *Schloss* of Berg, on Lake Starnberg—an eight-hour drive from Neuschwanstein —which was to be made over into a one-patient mental hospital.

The last of Ludwig's pathetic story will never be known for certain. The day after the arrival at Berg, Ludwig, who was behaving in a fairly quiet and docile manner, consented to go for an evening walk along the lakeside with Dr. Gudden. Neither was ever seen alive again. Through a misunderstanding, no attendant followed the two: the doctor had apparently expected to be followed at a discreet distance, while the attendant had understood that he was not to come at all. The body of Dr. Gudden was found in shallow water; he had drowned, and there were bruises and marks of strangulation on his neck. The body of the King was found farther out in the lake, in water less than four feet deep. He had been an excellent swimmer, so whether he had drowned himself or had suffered a heart attack and collapsed in the water will always be a mystery. A wooden cross, often garlanded with fresh flowers, marks the place where he died.

Mary Cable is an American writer now living in Southern Rhodesia. Her articles for HORIZON *include "The Grand Seraglio" for May, 1959, and "A Brilliance in the Bush," which appeared in November, 1960.*

The Wacky World of Tomi Ungerer

By WILLIAM COLE

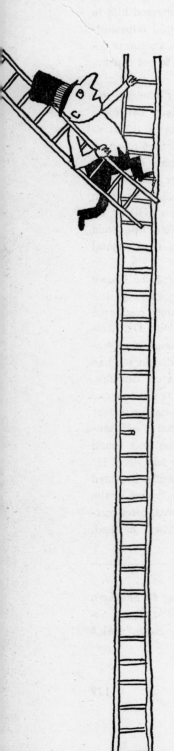

Tomi Ungerer and his wife, Miriam, have recently bought a very old, very small house in Greenwich Village. It is a house full of antiques and oddities: phrenological heads, old European and American posters, iron toys, shadow boxes, children's games from a century ago, and a small animal he has made from a stuffed sock and an electric-light fuse. When the mood is on him, he will fetch it for guests, leading it gently into the room on a string, talking to it and creating, with the nodding of its head and the movement of its body, a distinct and eerie feeling that it is alive.

It is Tomi's special genius that he can make anything in the field of graphics come wonderfully alive. Creative fervor is at a permanent boiling point within him; his imagination has the fecundity of a shad. He is at ease, and immensely productive, as a cartoonist, caricaturist, illustrator (and author) of children's books, advertising designer, book-jacket illustrator, and paper sculptor. This wide-ranging gift for handling anything that can be put on paper or done with paper has made him, in the four short years since he burst upon New York, the *Wunderkind* of the graphics world.

He was born Jean Tomi Ungerer in Strasbourg, France, in 1931. His first strong interest was geology, which he studied with intense concentration until the wanderlust peculiar to so many European youths struck him and he shrugged into his knapsack and hitchhiked all over the Continent, working for a spell on Scandinavian fishing boats. In 1953 he signed up for his military service with, as *Who's Who* puts it, "Mounted Police, Sahara." The mounts were camels.

Tomi came to the United States in 1957. He had settled on art as his métier and New York as his scene. Needing money to live on, he headed first for Madison Avenue. Such is the quality of his work and personality that people began delightedly to "discover" him and pass him on to others. For the past two years the agencies have been knocking on *his* door.

For almost any other artist a major advertising campaign is a matter of grave concern: each drawing wrings his artistic soul. He must sit down and think. He looks out the window. He makes sketches, roughs, and color tests. He winds up his inspiration. It is a major production. Not so with Tomi. Give him an assignment, turn away for a moment to dial a number, and bang, he's there with a dozen sketches! It is a legend among the agencies that he once did a full campaign for a major advertiser while standing at the Art Director's desk.

He has written and illustrated (in record time) seven books for small children, one of which, *Crictor*, surprised the librarians

of the country by making a boa constrictor popular. His other celebrated creation is the Mellops, a group of bumbling and lovable French pigs.

Tomi's paper sculpture has been exhibited in a New York show along with the work of the masters of this special art. He deals particularly in cards which, when opened, might reveal to the startled eye a protruding tongue, a laughing chicken, or the gaping, moving jaws of a fierce crocodile. In montage his special delight is to clip from a newspaper or catalog a photograph of an everyday object and, with a few strokes of his pen, to turn it into something utterly foreign. I have seen him, at the seashore, spend hours making gorgeous sleeping nudes of sand, twigs, and sea shells.

For the Christmas trade Atheneum Publishers brought out a lavish ten-dollar gallimaufry of his best work, bearing the typical Tomi title, *Horrible*, and the even more typical subtitle, "An Account of the Sad Achievements of Progress." Some of its offerings may prove distasteful to the genteel; Tomi delights in the vulgar and the macabre. He sees that vulgarity—sexual, social, and commercial—is everywhere about us. So why ignore it? He knows that small pains, exaggerations, and embarrassments are the basis for most humor, so he carries all these things further. Much of the world is foolish, cruel, and stupid. He thinks it proper to say so. He savors the grotesque and gruesome with what can only be called a wholesome appreciation. He responds to such unsual gifts as an undertaker's manual or an illustrated book on artificial limbs with pleased exclamations: "Look at thees peekture! Eets dees*gusting*!" His enthusiasm is not always shared.

Tomi's characters, in his cartoons and advertisements, are for the most part annonymous; they all look pretty much alike. They are little potty men with bulbous noses, and plump, bubbly-breasted women. They are parts of a composition, not the focus. When they must show expression to point up the drawing, they do, and they're funny; but most of the humor is in their bodies. His knowledge of anatomy—the twist of an arm, the defeated slope of a back, the pose of a dancer—is masterful. He draws as easily as a child does, without hesitation, knowing exactly where he wants the line to flow, his pen keeping up with his mind. In 1959 *Graphis* magazine quoted him as saying, "I can't delay, I must finish immediately and go on to the next . . . and the next."

The portfolio which follows presents some of Ungerer's work and, in photographs, Ungerer himself. It would be hard to say which is the more imaginative creation.

Ungerer outside his house in Greenwich Village

THOMAS HOPKER—RAPHO-GUILUMETTE

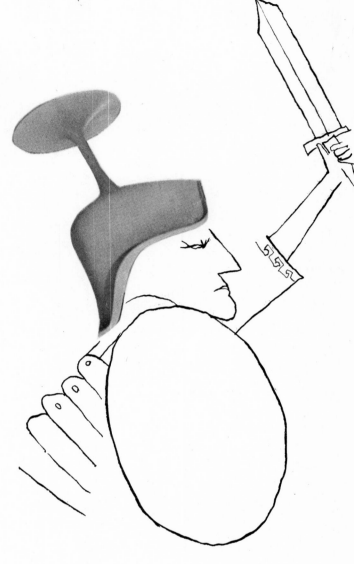

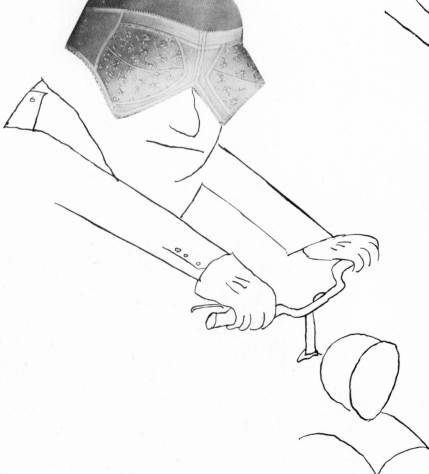

Tomi's eye (seen peering through the mask at the top of this page) is ever on the lookout for objects to inspire his drawings. With scissors and pen he then creates imaginative, sometimes gruesome, works such as these, which appear in his new book Horrible: *a general with rib-cage headdress, a brassière-goggled motorist, a Roman gladiator in Saarinen-chair helmet, and—something new in Gallic tortures—a guillotine for meatballs.*

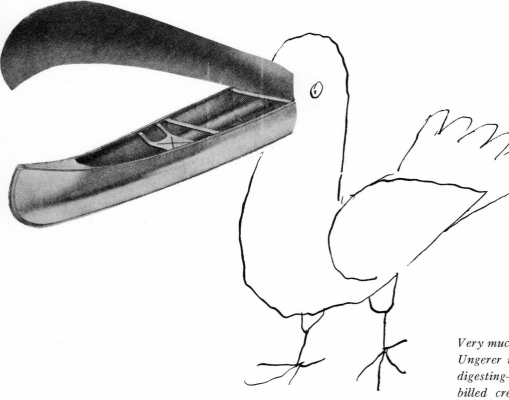

FROM *Horrible* BY TOMI UNGERER

Very much a part of the topsy-turvy world he draws, Ungerer is seen here in his studio designing—and digesting—a pasteboard chicken dinner. The canoe-billed creature at left is a bird of still another feather, a favorite subject in his private menagerie.

PHOTOGRAPHS LENI ISELIN

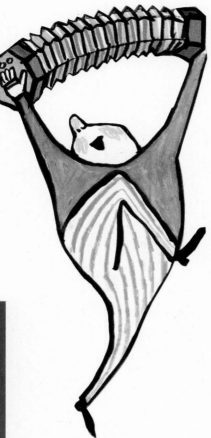

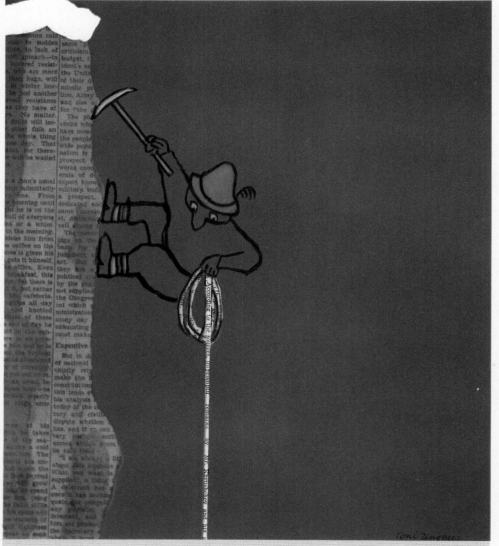

Why are so many New York Times
reporters going to the summit?

Because it is there!

*Tomi Ungerer as ad man is a believer in
the virtues of the amusing but to-the-
point sell. The drawings on this page
were done for national magazine and
poster campaigns, one to dramatize the
restorative effects of pep pills, the other
to promote the New York Times. Tomi's
stunning, almost childlike sense of color
and design also find expression in straight-
forward illustration, as in the evoca-
tive sketch of a French park, opposite.*

non vieux kiosque a musique

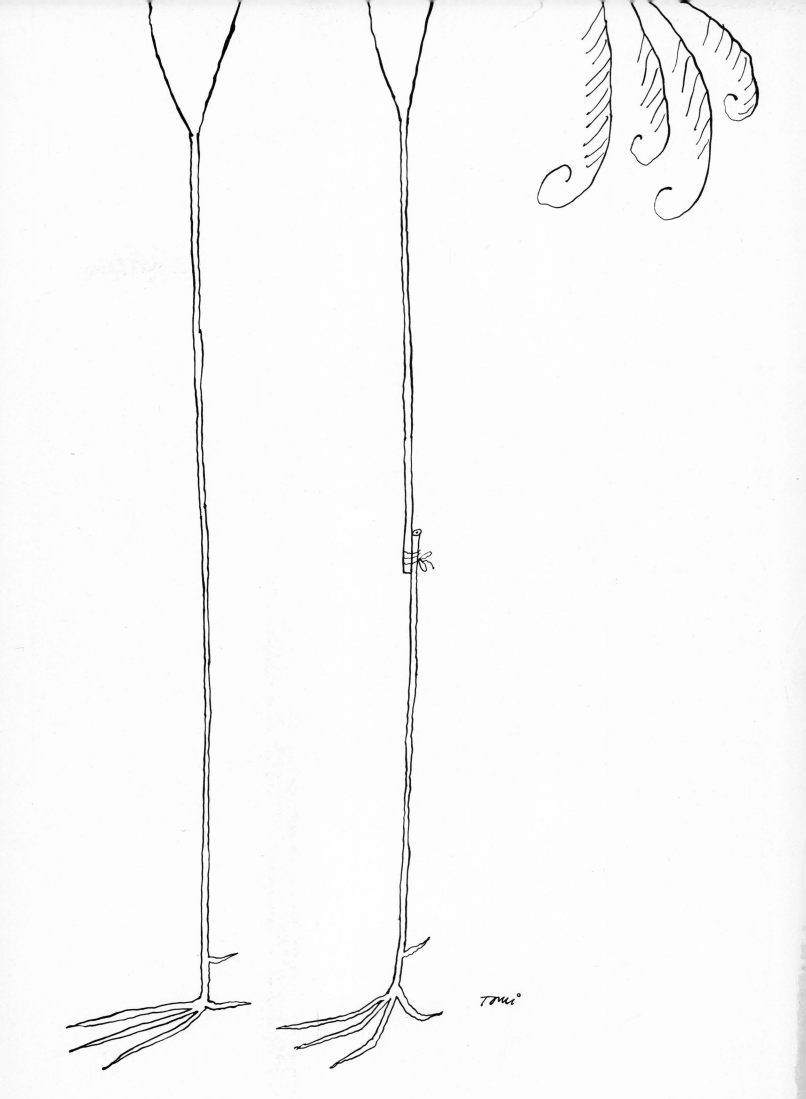